God in the Manger

God in the Manger

The Miraculous Birth of Christ

JOHN MACARTHUR

W PUBLISHING GROUP

www.wpublishinggroup.com

A Division of Thomas Nelson, Inc.
www.ThomasNelson.com

GOD IN THE MANGER

Copyright © 2001 W Publishing Group. All rights reserved.

Published by W Publishing Group, a unit of Thomas Nelson, Inc.,
P. O. Box 141000, Nashville, Tennessee 37214. No portion of this
book may be reproduced, stored in a retrieval system, or transmitted
in any form or by any means—electronic, mechanical, photocopy,
recording, or other—except for brief quotations in printed reviews,
without the prior permission of the publisher.

Unless otherwise indicated, Scripture quotations used in this book
are from The New King James Version (NKJV), copyright © 1979,
1980, 1982, Thomas Nelson, Inc., Publishers.

Scripture references marked NASB are from the New American
Standard Bible (NASB), copyright © 1960, 1977, 1995
by the Lockman Foundation.

Library of Congress Cataloging-in-Publication Data

ISBN 0-8499-5557-2

Printed in the United States of America

01   02   03   04   05   PHX   5   4   3   2   1

Contents

Introduction

❦

SURELY THE MOST WIDELY CELEBRATED HOLIDAY around the world each year—generating more attention, more excitement, and more anticipation from people than any other special day—is Christmas. Thanks to the huge amount of advertising and publicity that promotes the holiday with seemingly greater intensity and duration from one season to the next, Christmas has transcended national and cultural barriers.

Most people celebrate Christmas; but so few men and women understand what and whom it really commemorates. They probably have heard that it marks the birth of a great teacher from centuries ago; that they should emulate Him by promoting peace, good will, and charity during the Christmas season; and that they should strive to make the holiday less materialistic and more family oriented. But so many people, even Christians, never pause to fully consider the One who is at the center of the holiday. And so few ever truly grasp the historical and theological significance of what occurred that first Christmas.

Christmas commemorates a divine event and a divine person—the miraculous birth of the Son of God, Jesus Christ. Unlike most of our holidays, Christmas is not a celebration of an event strictly from human history that commemorates a human achievement or recognizes a national milestone. An authentic celebration of Christmas honors the most wonderful of divine accomplishments. It recognizes that the eternal, sovereign God came to earth as a human being to live a righteous life among His people and then to die as a perfect sacrifice to deliver from the wrath of God all who repent and believe.

With those truths in mind, we dare not trivialize or sentimentalize the persons and events surrounding the birth of Christ. We dare not ignore the significance of who He is and what He accomplished on behalf of sinners. And we must not hurry through the texts of familiar Christmas passages, thinking that just because we've read and heard them many times before, we know all they have to teach us. Therefore, I offer *God in the Manger: The Miraculous Birth of Christ* to provide you with a fresh perspective and, I trust, new insights into the greatest of all births.

We'll focus on the most well-known and beloved New Testament nativity narratives (Matt. 1–2 and Luke 1–2), along with a few relevant prophetic passages (Psalms, Isaiah, and Micah) as we delve into the historical reality of Jesus' incarnation.

The first two chapters consider important topics that people either misunderstand or overlook as they reflect on the birth of Christ. Chapter 1 confronts the virgin birth and demonstrates its crucial place in a biblical understanding of Jesus' person and work. Chapter 2 then analyzes the genealogies of our Lord and reveals their significance to the story of His birth.

The next five chapters begin to unfold the rich detail of Luke's incarnation narrative. Chapter 3 highlights the remarkable elements of the angel Gabriel's announcement to the youthful Mary. Chapter 4 tells how Mary's visit to her cousin Elizabeth confirmed the truth of Gabriel's announcement that Mary would bear the Messiah. In chapter 5, we consider the famous Luke 2 account of Jesus' birth in Bethlehem and see how certain world, national, and personal situations affected the story. In chapter 6, we'll chronicle the unusual appearance of the angels to the shepherds and discuss the monumental significance of their announcement. Then, in chapter 7, we'll see how the shepherds' reaction to the angels' proclamation parallels a typical conversion experience.

The next three chapters examine in detail some of the varied responses, positive and negative, that people had to news of Jesus' birth. Chapter 8 presents the responses of the Magi, King Herod, and the Jewish leaders, ranging from believing worship to disbelieving hostility to simple apathy, respectively. Chapter 9 demonstrates how Jesus' earthly parents responded as obedient and righteous witnesses when they presented Him to the Lord. Chapter 10 concludes this section with a careful examination of the venerable Simeon's prophetic words when he met the infant Christ near the Temple.

Finally, chapter 11 will seek to place our entire discussion into the proper theological context by looking at His birth from the divine perspective. There we'll thoroughly analyze Hebrews 1 to demonstrate convincingly that Jesus is indeed the Son of God.

If we have a clear understanding of the essential truths from Hebrews, we'll never lose sight of the reality that the Child in the Bethlehem manger was more than a sweet and innocent infant born in extraordinary circumstances—He was first and foremost the almighty God of the universe who humbly came to earth in human flesh to seek and to save the lost (Matt. 18:11; Luke 19:10; 5:32; Rom. 5:8).

1

The Amazing Fact of the Virgin Birth

Chapter One

The Amazing Fact of the Virgin Birth

EXTRAORDINARY BIRTHS are certainly not unprecedented in biblical history. As part of the Abrahamic Covenant, God promised to send a son to Abraham and Sarah (Gen. 17:19–22). They were both beyond normal childbearing ages and laughed at the prospect of being parents, yet they ultimately witnessed the miraculous arrival of their son, Isaac (Gen. 21:1–3). In Judges 13, an angel of the Lord told Manoah and his barren wife that they would have a special son. True to the heavenly messenger's words, Samson entered the world and for a time delivered the Israelites from the oppression of the Philistines.

Samuel, the first prophet, final judge, and anointer of kings, also demonstrated in his birth the providential power of God. He was the answer to the faithful, persevering prayers of his godly mother, Hannah, who had remained childless until then. John the Baptist's mother, Elizabeth, was also unable to have children until God graciously intervened when she was in her sixties or seventies and made her the mother of the forerunner of Christ (Luke 1:15–17, 76–79). But none of those special births was as amazing as the virgin birth of the Son of God, our Lord and Savior Jesus Christ.

UNBELIEF REGARDING THE VIRGIN BIRTH

Even though the fact of Jesus' virgin birth is clearly and concisely stated in Scripture, the unconverted mind of sinful humanity, as with all essential doctrines of the Christian faith, resists embracing the truth of His unique birth.

First of all, ancient mythologies and world religions counterfeited Christ's virgin birth with a proliferation of bizarre stories and inaccurate parallels. These stories undercut and minimized the uniqueness and profound impact of our Lord's birth. Several accounts illustrate the point. The Romans claimed that Zeus impregnated Semele without contact and produced Dionysus, lord of the earth. Babylonian religion asserted that a sunbeam in the priestess Semiramis conceived Tammuz, the Sumerian fertility god (Ezek. 8:14). Buddha's mother allegedly saw a large white elephant enter her belly when she conceived the deified Indian philosopher. Hinduism teaches that the divine Vishnu, after living as a fish, tortoise, boar, and lion, entered Devaki's womb and became her son, Krishna. Satan has propagated other similar legends, all with the purpose of undermining the nature of Christ's birth and deceiving people into seeing it as just another myth or nothing exceptional.

In addition, the scientific age and the emergence of modern and postmodern theologies during the past two centuries have eroded many professed believers' confidence in the reality of the virgin birth. (Along with that trend has been a noticeable decline in the percentage of "Christians" who believe in the deity of Christ.) But such skeptical thinking is foolish and directly contrary to the explicit teaching of all four Gospels, the Epistles, and the historical testimony of the entire early church that Jesus was none other than the virgin-born Son of God.

Unfortunately, a heart attitude of unbelief concerning Jesus' identity has characterized the majority of men and women since the Fall. The Jews who opposed Christ vividly illustrated that attitude on more than one occasion (John 5:18; 7:28–30; 10:30–39). But such hostility and lack of faith should not discourage us or deter us from embracing and defending the truth of Christ's virgin birth. The apostle Paul reminds us, "For what if some did not believe? Will their unbelief make the faithfulness of God without effect? Certainly not! Indeed, let God be true but every man a liar" (Rom. 3:3–4, 10:16; Isa. 53:1). The world's opinion, popular as it might be, is rarely a reliable source of truth.

Undoubtedly, therefore, the Holy Spirit acted with significant purpose in devoting an early passage from the Gospel of Matthew, at the front of the New Testament, to establish right away the humanity and deity of our Lord. His incarnation, properly understood, is foundational to Christianity. There could have been no genuine work of redemption apart from the fact of God becoming man and, by being both completely God and completely man, reconciling people to Himself through His substitutionary death and physical resurrection. If Jesus had not been both human and divine, there would be no gospel. (For further discussion on the necessity of believing and proclaiming the truth of Christ's virgin birth and deity, see chapter 8 of my book *Nothing but the Truth* [Wheaton, Ill.: Crossway, 1999]).

Many skeptical New Testament commentators will concede that Matthew and other authors of Scripture sincerely believed and taught that the Holy Spirit conceived Jesus without any assistance from a human father. But such interpreters nevertheless glibly discount the validity of Scripture's claims by immediately asserting that its writers were naive, uneducated, and subject to the myths and superstitions of ancient times. According to the critics, the Gospel writers merely adapted some of the familiar virgin birth legends to the story of Jesus' birth.

But nothing could be further from the truth. Matthew's account, for example, reads as history, but it is history he could know and record only because God revealed it and accomplished it by miraculous intervention. Matthew's words are far superior to the immoral and repulsive nature of the secular stories he and the other writers allegedly drew from. Here is his clear, uncomplicated narrative of the Incarnation:

Now the birth of Jesus Christ was as follows: After His mother Mary was betrothed to Joseph, before they came together, she was found with child of the Holy Spirit. Then Joseph her husband, being a just man, and not wanting to make her a public example, was minded to put her away secretly. But while he thought about these things, behold, an angel of the Lord appeared to him in a dream, saying, "Joseph, son of David, do not be afraid to take to you Mary your wife, for that which is conceived in her is of the Holy Spirit. And she will bring forth a Son, and you shall call His name Jesus, for He will save His people from their sins."

So all this was done that it might be fulfilled which was spoken by the Lord through the prophet, saying: "Behold, the virgin shall be with child, and bear a Son, and they shall call His name Immanuel," which is translated, "God with us."

Then Joseph, being aroused from sleep, did as the angel of the Lord commanded him and took to him his wife, and did not know her till she had brought forth her firstborn Son. And he called His name JESUS. (Matthew 1:18–25)

Matthew declares Jesus' divine lineage in this passage and reveals five aspects of His virgin birth: its first announcement, Joseph's response to it, the angel's clarification of it, its connection to prophecy, and its actual occurrence.

THE VIRGIN BIRTH ANNOUNCED

Matthew needs only one verse (1:18) to announce the fact of Christ's virgin birth. Such a concise statement, though it doesn't all by itself prove the point, strongly suggests that the notion of our Lord and Savior's virgin birth was not simply a man-made story. A human author, writing strictly on his own initiative, would characteristically tend to describe such a momentous and amazing event in an expansive, detailed, and elaborate manner. But not the apostle Matthew. He does relate additional circumstances surrounding the virgin birth, but the basic fact is stated in one simple sentence: "After His mother Mary was betrothed to Joseph, before they came together, she was found with child of the Holy Spirit."

Matthew devotes the previous seventeen verses to Jesus' human genealogy but just this part of one verse to His divine genealogy. As the Son of God, Jesus "descended" from His heavenly Father by a miraculous and never-repeated act of the Holy Spirit; even so, the Holy Spirit chose to announce that astounding truth by just one brief, declarative sentence. As all God's Word does, Matthew's simple statement contains the solemn tone of authenticity. By contrast, a human fabrication would tend to have that false ring of exaggeration to it, being filled out with much more "convincing" material than what this inspired version needed.

Scripture gives us little information about Mary and even less about Joseph. Mary was undoubtedly a godly young woman, probably a native of Nazareth who came from a relatively poor family. Joseph was the son of Jacob (Matt. 1:16) and was a craftsman, probably a carpenter (13:55). Most significant, he was a "just man" (1:19), one who placed saving trust in the coming Messiah.

Most likely Mary and Joseph were both quite young when they were engaged ("betrothed"). She may have been as young as twelve or thirteen, and he not any older than fifteen or sixteen. Such youthfulness at the time of a couple's engagement was standard for that culture. Another standard aspect of the Jewish betrothal was its binding nature—society considered the man and the woman legally married even though the formal ceremony and consummation might occur a year later. The purpose of the engagement period was to confirm each partner's fidelity when the two had little or no social contact with each another.

Mary and Joseph faithfully abstained from sexual relations with one another during the engagement period, as the contract required. That was also in accord with the Bible's high regard for sexual purity and

God's commands for sexual abstinence prior to the marriage ceremony and for sexual fidelity afterward. Thus, Mary's virginity was an important indicator of her godliness.

However, Mary's virginity protected something much more important than her own morality and godly reputation. It ensured the deity of Christ and supported the veracity of His teaching and works as the Son of God. Had Jesus been conceived by natural means, with Joseph or anyone else as His father, He would not have been God and would not have been a true Savior of sinners. To be in accord with what Scripture reported about His life, He would have had to make false claims about Himself, and He would have had to endorse false stories or hoaxes concerning the Resurrection and Ascension. Meanwhile everyone would have remained spiritually dead, condemned forever by their unforgiven sins. But we know that all that is absolutely contrary to what God's Word teaches.

The apostle Paul, for example, was also very clear and concise when he reiterated the true nature of the Incarnation: "But when the fullness of the time had come, God sent forth His Son, born of a woman" (Gal. 4:4). Paul includes no mention of a human father for Jesus because, according to the divine plan, God was His Father. Jesus had one human parent (Mary) so that He could be a man and identify closely with what it means to be human (Phil. 2:5–7; Heb. 4:15). And He had divine parentage so He could live a sinless life, perfectly fulfill the Law of God for us, and make the perfect sacrifice for our sins.

Admittedly, all these centuries after Matthew's divinely inspired Gospel declared that Jesus was born of a virgin, His miraculous conception remains impossible to understand by human reason alone. God chose not to explain the details of it to us, even as He chose to leave unexplained the intricacies of His creating the universe from nothing, the precise way He could be one God in three Persons, or exactly what happens when depraved sinners are born again as they repent of their sins and trust Christ. Many of the essentials of Christianity God wants believers to accept by faith. Full understanding will have to wait until heaven: "For now we see in a mirror, dimly, but then face to face. Now [we] know in part, but then [we] shall know [fully]" (1 Cor. 13:12).

JOSEPH'S RESPONSE TO THE VIRGIN BIRTH

Initial news of Mary's condition presented Joseph with a twofold problem. A caring and responsible person concerned about doing the right thing, Joseph was unwilling to proceed with his original plans once he perceived that a crucial part of those plans was no longer acceptable. His difficulty was intensified by the reality that he was a righteous man, genuinely concerned about doing what was morally and ethically right according to God's Law. First, when Joseph realized Mary was pregnant, he knew he could not go ahead with their marriage. He knew he was not the father and, based on what he knew at the time, he had to assume that another man was.

Joseph's second difficult decision concerned how he should then treat Mary. Because he was a good and loving man, he was grieved at the thought of shaming her publicly (a common practice in those days when a wife was unfaithful), and even more so at the prospect of demanding her death, as provided for in Deuteronomy 22:23–24. We don't know if he felt anger, resentment, or bitterness, but he certainly experienced shame at what he had to assume was true. However, Joseph's concern was not primarily with his own shame and embarrassment, but with Mary's. Matthew 1:19 says, "not wanting to make her a public example, [Joseph] was minded to put her away secretly."

Therefore, Joseph's plan was to divorce Mary secretly so she would not have to endure the disgrace of everyone in the community knowing about her supposed sin. Not many husbands ever display such firmly held and deeply felt love for their wives. Of course eventually, when the marriage didn't occur, everyone would have found out that something had gone wrong. But at least in the meantime Mary would be protected from humiliation and death.

The Lord, however, in His sovereign providence and wonderful grace, intervened directly into the situation and spared Joseph the further trauma of actually carrying out his divorce plans. "But while he thought about these things, behold, an angel of the Lord appeared to him in a dream, saying, 'Joseph, son of David, do not be afraid to take to you Mary your wife, for that which is conceived in her is of the Holy Spirit'" (Matt. 1:20). This verse underscores the miraculous nature of the virgin birth and the supernatural character surrounding the entire event of Christ's birth. It also provides divine assurance to Joseph ("son of David") and to us that Jesus had legitimate royal lineage that legally came through Joseph as a descendant of King David.

The angel's words provide the ultimate and most irrefutable testimony to the essential truth of the virgin birth and to the proper response Joseph was to have to Mary's extraordinary situation.

THE ANGEL CLARIFIES THE VIRGIN BIRTH

But what was the significance of Mary's pregnancy even though she had not had relations with Joseph or any other man? Joseph likely would have spent some time puzzling over that question if the divine messenger had not immediately clarified his pronouncement with these words, "'And she will bring forth a Son, and you shall call His name JESUS, for He will save His people from their sins'" (Matt. 1:21).

The angel tells Joseph that Mary will actually bear a son. And not just any son, but Jesus, who "will save His people from their sins." God chose the name Jesus for His Son because its basic meaning defined the fundamental, overarching purpose for the Son's coming to earth. *Jesus* is the Greek form of the Hebrew *Joshua, Jeshua,* or *Jehoshua,* each of which means "Jehovah (Yahweh) will save." The baby Mary had conceived by the power of the Holy Spirit and would give birth to in the plan of God would grow up to testify to the Father's salvation and would Himself be that salvation. By His own sacrificial death on the Cross and triumphant Resurrection from the grave He would save His own—all those who are drawn from sin to repentance and who receive faith to embrace His atoning work.

THE VIRGIN BIRTH PROPHESIED

At the time the angel told Joseph about Jesus' unique birth, the idea of a virgin birth was not one that was completely foreign to the Jews' understanding of their Scripture. Although they misinterpreted it, many of the rabbis exegeted Jeremiah 31:22 ("a woman shall encompass a man") in a way that suggested the Messiah would have an unusual birth. Their fanciful explanation of that verse ("Messiah is to have no earthly father," and "The birth of Messiah shall be like the dew of the Lord, as drops upon the grass without the action of man") at least preserved the general idea that the Messiah's birth would be unique.

Actually the Book of Genesis gives us the first glimpse that Christ's birth would be special: "'And I will put enmity between you and the woman, and between your seed and her Seed'" (3:15). Technically, the woman's seed belongs to the man, but Mary's impregnation by the Holy Spirit is the only instance in history that a woman had a seed within her that did not originate from a human man.

The later divine promise to Abraham concerned his "descendants" (Hebrew, "seed"; Gen. 12:7), a common Old Testament way of referring to offspring. The unique reference in Genesis 3:15 to "her Seed" looks beyond Adam and Eve to Mary and to Christ. The two seeds of that verse can have a twofold emphasis. First, they can primarily refer to all people who are part of Satan's progeny and all who are part of Eve's. The two groups constantly wage spiritual war against each other, with the people of righteousness eventually defeating the people of evil. Second, the word translated "Seed" can be singular and refer mainly to one final, glorious product of a woman—the Lord Jesus Himself, born without human seed. In that sense the prophecy is definitely Messianic.

Matthew 1:22–23 clearly identifies Jesus' virgin birth as a fulfillment of Old Testament prophecy: "So all this was done that it might be fulfilled which was spoken by the Lord through the prophet, saying: 'Behold, the virgin shall be with child, and bear a Son, and they shall call His name Immanuel,' which is translated, 'God with us.'" Matthew's quotation here of Isaiah 7:14 confirms that the prophet did in fact predict the virgin birth of Jesus Christ.

The prophet Isaiah made this momentous prophecy during the reign of Judah's wicked and idolatrous King Ahaz. The king faced a major military threat from the Israelite king, Pekah; and the Syrian king, Rezin; both of whom wanted to overthrow Ahaz and replace him with a more compliant monarch. Instead of seeking the Lord's help during that crisis, King Ahaz turned to Tiglath-Pileser, the brutal ruler of the pagan Assyrians. Ahaz even induced their assistance by offering them gold and silver stolen from God's Temple.

Ahaz refused to listen to Isaiah's report that God would deliver the people from Pekah and Rezin. Therefore the prophet spoke the remarkable prophecy of Isaiah 7:14, which told Ahaz that no one would destroy the people of God or the royal line of David. And sure enough, although Tiglath-Pileser destroyed the northern kingdom (Israel), deported its population, and overran Judah four times, God ultimately preserved His people just as He promised.

Isaiah also said that before another child (Maher-Shalal-Hash-Baz) was very mature or aware of events, the territories of Rezin and Pekah would be abandoned (Isa. 7:15–16). Again, the prophet's divinely inspired words were completely accurate. Before the other child, who was born to Isaiah's wife, was three years old, the two enemy kings were dead. Just as God fulfilled that ancient prophecy about Isaiah's son, so He was about to fulfill the one concerning the virgin birth of the Lord Jesus Christ. Both were signs from the Lord that He would not abandon His people, but the greatest of the two was obviously the second one: that His Son would actually be born of a virgin, live among His people, and die for their sins.

In his original pronouncement in 7:14, Isaiah used the Hebrew word *'alma* for "virgin." That is a significant term, and it's important to understand why the prophet used it. *'Alma* occurs six other times in the Old Testament (Gen. 24:43; Exod. 2:8; Ps. 68:25; Prov. 30:19; Song of Sol. 1:3; 6:8), and in each instance it connotes or denotes "virgin." Until recent times, both Jewish and Christian scholars always translated the word that way.

It is interesting that in modern Hebrew either *'alma* or *betula* can mean "virgin." However, Isaiah did not use *betula* because in Old Testament Hebrew it can refer to a married woman who is not a virgin (Deut. 22:19; Joel 1:8). It's apparent, therefore, that he used *'alma* in 7:14 with the clear, precise conviction that the woman who would bear the Messiah would indeed be a young woman who never had sexual relations with a man.

Matthew's use of Isaiah's prophecy followed directly in the prophet's path. The apostle was not giving *'alma* a Christian "twist" to make its usage fit a theory of the virgin birth. Instead, Matthew gave the term the same meaning as Isaiah intended, demonstrated by his translation of *'alma* with the Greek *parthenos,* the same word used by the Jewish translators of the Greek Old Testament.

Although the credibility of the virgin birth does not rest solely on the use of a Hebrew word, a general understanding of the background and usage of *'alma* strengthens our belief in Christ's unique birth. It also helps us to see that Matthew, under the inspiration of the Holy Spirit, knew exactly what he was doing when he related Isaiah 7:14 to the birth of Jesus and declared again the equally amazing truths that "the virgin shall be with child, and bear a Son, and they shall call His name Immanuel." In His virgin birth, Christ was, in the most literal sense, the Son who was "God with us."

THE OCCURRENCE OF THE VIRGIN BIRTH

All of Matthew's explanation of the significance of the virgin birth came within the revelatory dream God gave to Joseph. Such extraordinary, direct communication evidently occurred while Joseph engaged in the otherwise ordinary activity of sleeping. Matthew does not record any detail of Joseph's immediate reaction, except to say that he woke up and obeyed the angel's instructions: "Then Joseph, being aroused from sleep, did as the angel of the Lord commanded him and took to him his wife, and did not know her till she had brought forth her firstborn Son. And he called His name JESUS" (1:24–25).

You can imagine how great Joseph's feelings of amazement, relief, and gratitude must have been once he realized what the Lord, through the heavenly messenger, had told him. Not only could he go ahead and gladly take Mary as his wife with honor and righteousness, but also he could rejoice at the privilege of being allowed to bring up God's own Son.

The wedding ceremony of Joseph and Mary likely took place soon after Joseph received the angel's announcement. Matthew makes it clear that Mary remained a virgin until after Jesus was born, implying that normal marital relations began after that time. That, along with the references to Jesus' brothers and sisters (Matt. 12:46; 13:55–56; Mark 6:3), proves Mary was not a virgin for her entire life, as some claim.

Finally, Joseph followed through on God's command in Matthew 1:21 and named the baby Jesus, indicating, as we've already seen, that He was to be the Savior.

The amazing fact of Jesus' supernatural birth is the only way to explain the perfect, sinless life He lived while on earth. A skeptic who denied the virgin birth once asked a Christian, "If I told you that child over there was born without a human father, would you believe me?" "Yes," the believer replied, "if he lived as Jesus lived."

Christ's virgin birth is a necessary component that helps us believe and make sense of the entire story of His person and work. His extraordinary conception and birth, not before or since equaled, is an amazing reality that we should with joy and gratitude never take for granted.

2

A Look at Jesus' Family Tree

Chapter Two

⌘

A Look at Jesus' Family Tree

HAVE YOU GIVEN MUCH THOUGHT to your ancestry or the roots of your family tree lately? Probably not during the past few days or weeks. But chances are, if you're typical of most people, you or someone in your family has done some genealogical research during the past ten or fifteen years.

Many books, articles, and Internet sites are available to help us delve into our genealogical records and identify the famous, the infamous, and the merely obscure people of our ancestries. For a small but dedicated number of people, this activity has become an all-consuming obsession that helps them fill a psychological void in their lives or build up their self-esteem. But for most of us, it is little more than a nice curiosity or at best simply a recreation. And it can be an expensive activity if you travel back to your hometown to look up records and obituaries concerning your family members.

THE IMPORTANCE OF GENEALOGIES TO THE JEWS

To the Jews of Bible times, however, genealogies were extremely important. Interest in such matters went beyond the realm of curiosity, recreation, meeting psychological needs, or even consideration of family identity and religious solidarity (which we see with present-day groups such as the

Mormons). There were four major reasons that accurate and complete genealogies were so critical to the ancient Jews. And as you'll see in this chapter, two such genealogies were important to the story of Jesus' birth.

First, ancestry determined one's claim on land, based on the original tribal allocation of the land of Palestine. When the Israelites first settled in the Promised Land, God divided it into parcels for each tribe (Num. 26:52–56).

Second, ancestry determined claims to the right of inheritance. If a person claimed he had a right to property, servants, an estate, crops, or other material possessions, the validity of such claims was determined by the genealogies of those involved. For example, in Ruth 3–4, ancestry allowed for the transfer of property.

Third, ancestry in Israel established the basis of taxation. When Mary and Joseph went to be taxed in Luke 2, they traveled to Bethlehem because that was the hometown of David, and they were of the house and line of David. They were aware of their lineage because certainly their parents and other older relatives would have described how their family heritage went all the way back to King David. And though they were young, Mary and Joseph loved God and Scripture and surely knew what the prophets wrote concerning Messiah's relationship to the line of David. Based on that knowledge of Scripture and their family's genealogical records, which were kept in Bethlehem, Mary and Joseph made the journey to receive their tax assessment.

Last, and most important, any claim to the priesthood or royalty had to be verified by genealogy. In Ezra 2:61–63, for example, a number of men were excluded from the priesthood when the records did not verify their claims. Likewise, any claim to be king (and ultimately, Messiah) would be rejected if the one making the assertion could not prove he had direct lineage from the great king David himself.

Therefore, in the theocracy of Israel—a kingdom ruled by God, with its legal statutes outlined in Scripture and led by God-ordained priests and kings—genealogies were very critical. That's why the Jews kept careful, accurate, and fastidious genealogical records. The genealogies of Jesus Christ in the Gospels of Matthew and Luke reflect those characteristics. The writers' use of such records demonstrates not only that the Holy Spirit guided them, but also that they had access to actual, verifiable public records that proved the true and accurate genealogy of the Lord Jesus Christ. Jesus' genealogy makes a crucial contribution to His credentials as Messiah. If He is to be verified as the King, David's greater Son who will rule, He must have Davidic lineage.

THE TWO GENEALOGIES OF JESUS

The New Testament contains two lists that outline for us the genealogy of Christ. Matthew records his in Matthew 1:1–17, and Luke presents his in Luke 3:23–38. The apostle Matthew included his genealogy as the first part of his chronological account of the life of Jesus. By contrast, Luke waited until the end of the third chapter of his Gospel to include a genealogy of Jesus. He placed it between the accounts of Jesus' baptism and His Temptation as a key element of establishing the Messiah's credentials. There are also other differences between the two genealogies that are worth examining briefly.

The Differences in the Lists

First of all, the two genealogies take different chronological views of Jesus' family tree. Luke goes from the present to the past, beginning with Jesus' grandfather and going all the way back to Adam and God. Matthew, however, approaches matters in the opposite fashion. He goes from the past to the present, starting with Abraham and ending with Jesus.

Here are the two separate, but equally inspired and valid, versions of the genealogy of our Lord. Notice some of the differences as you read the two lists consecutively:

The book of the genealogy of Jesus Christ, the Son of David, the Son of Abraham:

Abraham begot Isaac, Isaac begot Jacob, and Jacob begot Judah and his brothers. Judah begot Perez and Zerah by Tamar, Perez begot Hezron, and Hezron begot Ram. Ram begot Amminadab, Amminadab begot Nahshon, and Nahshon begot Salmon. Salmon begot Boaz by Rahab, Boaz begot Obed by Ruth, Obed begot Jesse, and Jesse begot David the king.

David the king begot Solomon by her who had been the wife of Uriah. Solomon begot Rehoboam, Rehoboam begot Abijah, and Abijah begot Asa. Asa begot Jehoshaphat, Jehoshaphat begot Joram, and Joram begot Uzziah. Uzziah begot Jotham, Jotham begot Ahaz, and Ahaz begot Hezekiah. Hezekiah begot Manasseh, Manasseh begot Amon, and Amon begot Josiah. Josiah begot Jeconiah and his brothers about the time they were carried away to Babylon.

And after they were brought to Babylon, Jeconiah begot Shealtiel, and Shealtiel begot Zerubbabel. Zerubbabel begot Abiud, Abiud begot Eliakim, and Eliakim begot Azor. Azor begot Zadok, Zadok begot Achim, and Achim begot Eliud. Eliud begot Eleazar, Eleazar begot Matthan, and Matthan begot Jacob. And Jacob begot Joseph the husband of Mary, of whom was born Jesus who is called Christ.

So all the generations from Abraham to David are fourteen generations, from David until the captivity in Babylon are fourteen generations, and from the captivity in Babylon until the Christ are fourteen generations. (Matthew 1:1–17)

Now Jesus Himself began His ministry at about thirty years of age, being (as was supposed) *the* son of Joseph, *the son* of Heli, *the son* of Matthat, *the son* of Levi, *the son* of Melchi, *the son* of Janna, *the son* of Joseph, *the son of* Mattathiah, *the son* of Amos, *the son* of Nahum, *the son* of Esli, *the son* of Naggai, *the son* of Maath, *the son* of Mattathiah, *the son* of Semei, *the son* of Joseph, *the son* of Judah, *the son* of Joannas, *the son* of Rhesa, *the son* of Zerubbabel, *the son* of Shealtiel, *the son* of Neri, *the son* of Melchi, *the son* of Addi, *the son* of Cosam, *the son* of Elmodam, *the son* of Er, *the son* of Jose, *the son* of Eliezer, *the son* of Jorim, *the son* of Matthat, *the son* of Levi, *the son* of Simeon, *the son* of Judah, *the son* of Joseph, *the son* of Jonan, *the son* of Eliakim, *the son* of Melea, *the son* of Menan, *the son* of Mattathah, *the son* of Nathan, *the son* of David, *the son* of Jesse, *the son* of Obed, *the son* of Boaz, *the son* of Salmon, *the son* of Nahshon, *the son* of Amminadab, *the son* of Ram, *the son* of Hezron, *the son* of Perez, *the son* of Judah, *the son* of Jacob, *the son* of Isaac, *the son* of Abraham, *the son* of Terah, *the son* of Nahor, *the son* of Serug, *the son* of Reu, *the son* of Peleg, *the son* of Eber, *the son* of Shelah, *the son* of Cainan, *the son* of Arphaxad, *the son* of Shem, *the son* of Noah, *the son* of Lamech, *the son* of Methuselah, *the son* of Enoch, *the son* of Jared, *the son* of Mahalalel, *the son* of Cainan, *the son* of Enosh, *the son* of Seth, *the son* of Adam, *the son* of God. (Luke 3:23–38; italics inserted by NKJV translators)

I believe Luke's method gives his genealogy more of a dramatic element than Matthew's. By starting at the present and working back to the past, the beloved physician turned historian and theologian offers us a sense of wonder and excitement as we try to anticipate how far back his genealogy of Jesus will take us.

Matthew's list, on the other hand, is much more predictable as it starts with Abraham and traces the Messiah's line forward to Jesus. Matthew's goal in his list was to satisfy the Jews' concern about Messiah's legality. Judaism began with Abraham, the father of the nation of Israel. Therefore, it was only necessary to prove Messiah's credentials to the Jews by tracing His line from Abraham, through David, right down to Jesus. That's more specific than Luke's universal approach, which shows how Christ the Son of Man and Son of God links with all humanity clear back to Adam and finally to God Himself.

Between the two records there are also some differences in the names. First, Luke traces Jesus' line back to David through Nathan (3:31), David's third son born to Bathsheba. But Matthew traces Jesus' line back to David through Solomon (1:6), David's first son born to Bathsheba.

Second, Luke identifies Jesus' grandfather as Heli (3:23), whereas Matthew says that His grandfather was a man named Jacob (1:16). Finally, there are major differences in the genealogies going from David to Christ. Whereas the lists of names are identical from David to Abraham, the two are completely different when you work your way from David to the Lord Jesus.

Explaining the Differences in the Lists

It's amazing that people often struggle to explain the differences in the two genealogies. But it's not really that difficult, and there is certainly no problem with having two genealogies for Jesus. In Matthew, the genealogy is paternal, going through Jesus' earthly father, Joseph; and Joseph's father, Jacob; back to David. In Luke, the genealogy is maternal, going through Jesus' mother, Mary; and Mary's father, Heli; back to David.

When you look at the genealogies this way, the reason for the differences is clear. Everyone has two genealogies—one paternal and one maternal. And Jesus, like everyone, had a paternal and maternal grandfather. So essentially Jesus' family tree, in exhibiting certain basic differences, follows the pattern of every human genealogy. That is the simplest way to account for the discrepancies in the names.

The necessity to establish His legal right to the throne of David is another very important reason the two Gospel writers gave us two different forms of Jesus' family tree. And that legal right came through the father; therefore, Matthew's paternal genealogy proved that Jesus came from a line that proceeded from David through Solomon. That proof is true even though Jesus was not the human son of Joseph. Because Joseph married Mary, the mother of Jesus, he became the legal father of Jesus. As a result, Jesus received from Joseph the full legal right to the throne of David.

Luke's maternal genealogy further solidifies Jesus' claim to the throne of David by proving that He has the blood of David in His veins because of His mother, Mary. So, either way, Jesus is a genuine, legitimate descendant of King David.

The Messiah is king legally through Joseph and naturally through Mary. His scriptural credentials are thorough, clear, and irrefutable. From every perspective, we can crown Jesus King of kings and Lord of lords.

Critical Reactions to the Lists

The two genealogical lists have certainly been the unfair targets of doubt, questioning, and disbelief during the past two centuries by so-called scholarly critics of the Gospels. And that has been true for all portions of Scripture. But any in-depth discussion of such matters is outside the scope and purpose of this book. However, I do find it interesting how Jesus' contemporary critics and opponents among the Jewish leaders responded to what His genealogies concluded.

The Pharisees, Sadducees, high priests—and all the enemies of Christ—sought to discredit Him as their Messiah. The thought that Jesus of Nazareth, the son of plain folks like Joseph and Mary, was their Messiah was offensive to them, and that's why they ultimately had Him killed.

That's why Jesus' foes did everything possible to dishonor Him and disqualify Him from His Messianic claim. And it's certainly reasonable to assume that, soon after the Lord made that claim, the Jewish leaders scrambled to find the official scroll containing His genealogical information. They would have had to make just a short trip south of Jerusalem to the town of Bethlehem, where the lineages and tax records for the line of David were kept. Once they got hold of those records, they could have determined rather quickly if Joseph and Mary's ancestry really was Davidic. And discovering that Jesus didn't actually belong to the line of David would have been all His opponents needed to discredit Him as Messiah. Even though Jesus did numerous miracles, preached and taught persuasively, and claimed to be sent from the Father, discovering that He was not an ancestor of David would have been enough to disprove His Messianic claim.

However, it's striking that a study of the entire New Testament does not once report anyone claiming that Jesus didn't come from David. As much as Jesus' enemies may have wanted to make His ancestry an issue, they never did. That's because the records supported His claim to be the Son of David. So there was never an official denial that Jesus was from the Davidic line. In fact, here is what the crowds exclaimed during the Passover season just before Jesus' death, when He made His triumphal entry into Jerusalem (the day we commonly call Palm Sunday): "'Hosanna to the Son of David! Blessed is He who comes in the name of the LORD!' Hosanna in the highest!'" (Matt. 21:9). There was simply no denying our Lord's rightful ancestry and position of highest honor.

HIGHLIGHTS OF LUKE'S GENEALOGY

Luke's presentation of Jesus' family tree, using the names of His maternal line, contains several fascinating details and highlights. First of all, the opening verse of the genealogy includes the significant expression, "being (as was supposed) the son of Joseph" (3:23). That is a way of saying that Jesus was not actually the son of Joseph and therefore by implication that He was the son of Mary. Luke used "(as was supposed) the son of Joseph" to conform to the classic genealogical style of referring solely to male relatives. He wanted to maintain that format for his readers, and yet, by this implicit reference to Mary, he emphasized that his genealogy would follow the maternal line. All of that counters any erroneous notion that Jesus' genealogy could only be paternal to be valid. But just as important, by indicating that Jesus was not the physical son of Joseph, Luke is once again affirming the Savior's virgin conception and birth.

Another distinctive of Luke's genealogical format is worthy of mention. If you look at Luke 3:23–38 in a copy of the New King James Version of the Bible (or the NKJV quotation of that passage earlier in our chapter), you'll notice that in front of all the names but one, "the son" is italicized. That means the Greek text omitted all those occurrences. Only before Joseph's name does "son" appear in the original. But why did Luke structure his genealogy that way?

The answer is not that complicated. Luke wanted to separate Joseph's name from the rest of the genealogy. Actually verse 23 should more literally read like this: "Jesus Himself, the son of Joseph (as was supposed), began His ministry at about thirty years of age, being of Heli." This rendering allowed the original readers to jump directly from Jesus to His earthly grandfather, Heli, the father of Mary. Thus Luke maintained, as he preferred, the classic male-names-only format to the genealogy and still underscored that the genealogy was truly Mary's.

Luke's version of Jesus' family tree contains another interesting feature: Many of the names are unfamiliar to us. From Heli back to Nathan, the only names we recognize or know anything about from elsewhere in Scripture are Zerubbabel and Shealtiel, two leaders of the Jews who returned from the Exile in Babylon. The other names were common Hebrew names in ancient times, and we can trust that they belong in the genealogy as the actual names of Jesus and Mary's forebears. However, the Holy Spirit did not deem it necessary for us to know anything about the individuals. Only in the section from David to Adam do we find predominantly familiar names that we can also find recorded in the Old Testament.

The final question you may be inclined to ask in view of Luke's detailed genealogy is, "So why all of this?" The answer is simple. A general awareness of the details of Christ's genealogy helps us appreciate the God-ordained credentials for the person of our Lord and Savior. Four basic elements of Luke's genealogy summarize those credentials.

First and most important, Luke asserts that Jesus is the Son of God (3:38). Adam was the original son of God by creation, and he fully bore the divine image unmarred, unspoiled, unpolluted, and uncorrupted until he fell into sin. When that happened, the initial image of God in humanity was shattered, and every one of Adam's descendants has been stained by his original sin and born with a corrupted image of God. But Jesus came into the world fully pleasing to God, as the kind of man Adam once was—sinless, bearing an absolutely perfect image of the Father, and obeying His will in every respect. As God said in Luke 3:22, " 'You are My beloved Son; in You I am well pleased.' "

Second, Luke's genealogy makes it clear that Jesus is a Son of Adam. While on earth, He was fully human. And just like His followers, He was tempted, troubled, persecuted, hated, reviled, and subjected to all the normal difficulties of life (Heb. 4:15). Like Adam, Christ descended from a higher plane to a lower plane; but unlike Adam, He descended into obedience, not disobedience (Phil. 2:5–8). Nevertheless, He was every bit of what Adam was—fully human, fully attached to the earth as the Son of Man. And Jesus was also firmly connected to heaven as the Son of God. Thus, Luke affirms that Jesus in His incarnation was at the same time fully God and fully man—the Son of God as to His deity and the Son of Adam as to His humanity.

Last, Luke's genealogy attests to a third and fourth truth about the person of Jesus. Ethnically, He was the Son of Abraham. That is, He was and is the promised Seed. When God made a promise to Abraham, it was to a Seed: "Now to Abraham and his Seed were the promises made. He does not say, 'And to seeds,' as of many, but as of one, 'And to your Seed,' who is Christ" (Gal. 3:16). Christ is the promised Seed who will bring about all the Abrahamic blessings. And, as we have already discussed, concerning royalty Christ is the Son of David. He is the promised King who will usher in the glory of all the Davidic promise.

The family tree of Jesus Christ consists of far more than two lists of ancient Hebrew names. It is also much more than boring paternal and maternal lists of Jesus' earthly ancestors. It is a wonderful testimony to God's grace and to His Son's earthly ministry. Jesus was born the friend of sinners, as He stated in his admonishment to the Jewish leaders: "'I have not come to call the righteous, but sinners, to repentance'" (Luke 5:32). The Messiah presented in the genealogies is truly the Lord of grace.

3

The Angel's Announcement to Mary

Chapter Three

❧

The Angel's Announcement to Mary

THANKS TO THE INCREASINGLY PERVASIVE ROLE of the mass media, people of every generation during the twentieth century heard some very memorable, and at times unexpected, news announcements. Such declarations, both print and broadcast, concerned crucial events that shaped the history of the century. For example, a few people still remember the newspaper extras of November 11, 1918 that heralded the end of World War I. A few more will recall the dramatic and exhilarating headlines of May 1927 that said Charles Lindbergh had officially completed his daring attempt to be the first aviator to fly solo across the Atlantic. Even more folks can remember the somber news of September 1939—the beginning of World War II in Europe—and December 7, 1941—the surprise bombing of Pearl Harbor and American entrance into the war. Many more will remember what they were doing on November 22, 1963 or January 28, 1986 when they first heard the shocking bulletins that President John F. Kennedy had died from gunshots or that the entire crew of the space shuttle Challenger had died when the craft exploded shortly after liftoff.

As huge, staggering, and widely proclaimed as those modern news announcements were, each is almost inconsequential when compared to the startling and far-reaching announcement of Jesus Christ's birth, which Mary heard from the angel Gabriel. That simple, lovely, unmistakably clear narrative explicitly features the divine character of the event. There is no more miraculous, compelling announcement in all of history than that which opens Luke's familiar and beloved account of the birth of our Lord:

> Now in the sixth month the angel Gabriel was sent by God to a city of Galilee named Nazareth, to a virgin betrothed to a man whose name was Joseph, of the house of David. The virgin's name was Mary. And having come in, the angel said to her, "Rejoice, highly favored one, the Lord is . with you; blessed are you among women!"
>
> But when she saw him, she was troubled at his saying, and considered what manner of greeting this was. Then the angel said to her, "Do not be afraid, Mary, for you have found favor with God. And behold, you will conceive in your womb and bring forth a Son, and shall call His name JESUS. He will be great, and will be called the Son of the Highest; and the Lord God will give Him the throne of His father David. And He will reign over the house of Jacob forever, and of His kingdom there will be no end. (Luke 1:26–33)

This is the angel's promise that God was coming into the world, but it's not the first time God made such a promise. Gabriel's announcement actually heralded the beginning of the promise's fulfillment. The monumental news of the Incarnation broke with supernatural surprise to Mary and soon dispelled the mundane tedium that was human history at that time. The news was part of God's plan of redemption, which He devised even before the creation of the world. And the Holy Spirit previewed that plan from the opening of Scripture, at the start of human history. God originally established the hope of a Savior in Genesis 3:15, and the divine authors of the Old Testament kept it alive for millennia in the hearts of believers (Gen. 49:10; Deut. 18:15; Ps. 2:6–12; Isa. 7:14; 9:6–7; 52:13–53:12; Dan. 2:45; 7:13–14; 9:26; Mic. 5:2).

The Old Testament is filled with prophecies and promises concerning the coming Messiah (approximately 350). At the end of Luke's Gospel, when the risen Jesus walked on the road to Emmaus with several disciples, Luke records the following interaction: "'O foolish ones, and slow of heart to believe in all that the prophets have spoken! Ought not the Christ to have suffered these things and to enter into His glory?' And beginning at Moses and all the Prophets, He expounded to them in all the Scriptures the things concerning Himself" (Luke 24:25–27).

So it's clear that the angel's words to Mary are part of the fulfillment of God's ancient promises. Those words possess a striking and unmistakable quality of simplicity—yet there is enough wonder and amazement in the announcement's basic elements so that any open-minded person ought to embrace them and exult over their reality.

THE DIVINE MESSENGER

The best way to grasp the significance of the angel's announcement is to look at it from God's perspective. Everything about the proclamation was divine, including first of all its divine messenger. That God would send a message by means of a holy angel—and for the second time in less than a year (Luke 1:11–20)—was in itself amazing. God's people had not seen or heard from an angel in more than four hundred years. During that time there had been no revelation from the Lord, no miracle, and certainly no sequence of miracles. But then for the second time in the span of a few months the same angel appeared, both times with an extraordinary birth announcement to an ordinary person.

Luke 1:26 identifies the divine messenger as Gabriel, the same angel who came a few months earlier to the priest Zacharias with news about John the Baptist's birth.

Gabriel is one of only two angels who are actually named in the Bible. The other one, Michael, is a superangel, associated with assignments requiring power and strength. Gabriel is God's supreme messenger, who brought great, glorious, and crucial announcements from heaven. In Daniel 9, for example, he delivered the all-important pronouncement to

Daniel regarding the rest of redemptive history, as unfolded in the incredible vision of the seventy weeks. And now the message of Christ's forthcoming birth was so critically important that Gabriel again announced it.

Gabriel delivered the most astounding and significant birth announcement ever. And it was even more incredible because he brought it directly from the throne of God. Luke 1:19 says, "'I am Gabriel, who stands in the presence of God.'" This high-ranking angel of God came down out of heaven to a Galilean town called Nazareth. And that town, population several thousand, was quite obscure to the outside world. Galilee, an official region north of Jerusalem, was recognizable to most people; therefore, Luke gave his readers a better idea of the town where Christ would grow up by identifying it by regional location.

One of the remarkable facts about Galilee's role in the story of Jesus' birth is that the region was not the center of Jewish culture and religion. In fact, it tended to be more Gentile in its orientation, with a significant non-Jewish population surrounding the area. That's why the district north of Jerusalem was called Galilee of the Gentiles. It's quite intriguing that when God made the direct, formal announcement of the coming of His Son, the promised Jewish Messiah and King, it came to a part of Israel that was intersected by many Gentiles. We can almost paraphrase God's intention this way: "My Son will come to a family from Nazareth in Galilee, because He will be the Savior not only of all Jews who believe, but also of believers from every tribe, tongue, and nation."

THE PERSON OF DIVINE CHOICE

Luke's account of Christ's birth announcement continues its divine perspective by reporting God's choice of the special person who would be Jesus' mother. That person is identified as "a virgin betrothed to a man whose name was Joseph, of the house of David. The virgin's name was Mary" (1:27).

Not only did the Father send an angel to a small, obscure town in Galilee, to one specific house—He also chose one of its residents to have a major role in the birth of Jesus. That person was a young teenager named Mary. The name *Mary* is the Greek form of the Hebrew *Miriam* and means "exalted one." Beyond that, we know virtually nothing about Mary's background, because the Bible does not tell us anything. (For a profile of Mary, see chapter 7 of my book *In the Footsteps of Faith* [Wheaton, Ill.: Crossway Books, 1998].)

In Luke's account, "virgin" is the Greek word *parthenos,* meaning "one who has had no sexual relations." As we alluded to in chapter 1 of this study, the term was never used of a married woman. So we can be certain that Mary was truly a virgin. And in that regard, Mary's marital status followed the normal Jewish practice, which was in turn patterned after Roman law of that day. Girls were engaged at twelve or thirteen years of age (around the time of reaching puberty) and married at the end of the engagement period. That practice ensured that adolescent girls maintained their virginity until marriage.

When you think about it, God's sovereign choice of Mary to be the mother of Jesus is most astonishing. Out of all the women He could have chosen—queens, princesses, sisters or daughters of the wealthy and influential—He chose an unknown, unassuming young woman named Mary from an obscure village called Nazareth. But God's plans and purposes often do not unfold in the manner we, as humans, would have selected.

THE DIVINE BLESSING TO MARY

As amazing as any announcement's messenger might be, and as fascinating as the identity of the primary recipient is, the most important aspect of any announcement—what people really want to know—is the content. And the content of most everyday pronouncements is usually fairly mundane, often striking us as boring and uninspiring. That is certainly not true regarding the introductory content of Gabriel's announcement.

Luke 1:28–30 confirms that the angel's incredible message is indeed from God and contains His blessing: "And having come in, the angel said to her, 'Rejoice, highly favored one, the Lord is with you; blessed are you among women!' But when she saw him, she was troubled at his saying, and considered what manner of greeting this was. Then the angel said to her, 'Do not be afraid, Mary, for you have found favor with God.'"

In keeping with Luke's simple, unadorned narration, Gabriel merely entered the house and greeted Mary with a benign "hello" (usually translated "hail" or "rejoice"). Mary, who was apparently alone and preparing food at the time, must have received the angel's greeting as a definite understatement. But there was a reason the greeting did not come with elaborate heavenly fanfare or intense drama. Divine wisdom undoubtedly knew a low-key introduction would prevent Mary from panicking. After all, she had never seen an angel before; and such a phenomenon could have frightened her, since she was an inexperienced youth. So a calm, reassuring, human-style voice was best for this most special situation.

Gabriel's next statement clearly and immediately revealed that the divine blessing sovereignly bestowed on Mary was nothing less than God's grace. However, for centuries the Roman Catholic Church has not embraced that truth, but instead has misled its adherents by accepting the Latin Vulgate Bible's inaccurate translation of Luke 1:28. During that time, Catholic commentators, writers, and theologians have propagated the familiar but wrong rendering, "Hail, Mary, full of grace." That has led millions to accept the seriously erroneous belief that Mary is the source of immeasurable grace, which she bestows on others.

Simply reading and understanding the entirety of Gabriel's opening statement easily refutes that heresy: "'highly favored one, the Lord is with you; blessed are you among women!'. . . 'you [Mary] have found favor with God'" (vv. 28, 30). Those words are not praising Mary for her inherently virtuous, godly, or worthy character. The angel's message to her simply said that God had freely chosen to give grace to Mary—that is what made her favored and blessed.

Gabriel had to use such an expression because, before God, Mary was unworthy in her own strength. That means she was a sinner, and sinners need God's grace. In that sense, Mary was just like you and me—she had no grace to dispense, because she needed the saving grace only God can give. Therefore, she was the recipient of grace, not the source or bestower of it.

Mary did not respond with pride or smug self-satisfaction, as the Catholic view might suggest, but instead she reacted to Gabriel's statement with humility and perplexed pondering. "But when she saw him, she was troubled at his saying, and considered what manner of greeting this was" (v. 29). The angel's appearance did not shake Mary as much as did the nature of his words. "Considered" refers to a state of mind that is disturbed, confused, and perplexed. But why would Mary have reacted that way to the message? Simply because she knew she was a sinner who did not deserve to receive God's grace. That's why later she praised God and called Him, "God my Savior" (v. 47).

Mary knew what all righteous, believing people know—that she needed a Savior. And that is probably the best indication we have that Mary was a true believer. All genuinely righteous people are distressed when they face God (or in Mary's case, one of His holy angels) because they know they're sinners. As she pondered Gabriel's message, Mary very well may have asked herself over and over, *Why would God ever want to choose me, an unworthy sinner, to be the recipient of His amazing grace? Why would the Lord single out me for such special privilege?* To her, it was staggering; nothing on earth could have prepared her for such a breathtaking opening announcement.

Even though Mary's primary response to Gabriel's words was one of perplexity and serious pondering, she also reacted with fear. Such supernatural appearances always generated a certain amount of fear and trembling in the human witnesses (Luke 1:13; 2:10). Therefore, it was appropriate that the angel would give Mary some words of assurance: "'Do not be afraid, Mary, for you have found favor with God'" (1:30). Gabriel was not coming to Mary in judgment, so there was nothing for her to fear.

God affirmed that He had extended His grace to Mary for no other reason than it suited His good pleasure and perfect plan. The issue was not Mary's individual worthiness or human merit; it was God's sovereign choice. God exercised the same prerogative centuries earlier when He spared Noah and his family from the Flood: "But Noah found grace in the eyes of the LORD" (Gen. 6:8).

Mary later acknowledged God's incredible grace and mercy toward her: "'My soul magnifies the Lord, and my spirit has rejoiced in God my Savior. For He has regarded the lowly state of His maidservant; for behold, henceforth all generations will call me blessed. For He who is mighty has done great things for me, and holy is His name'" (Luke 1:46–49). She uttered those words of praise, not as the "blesser," but as the "blessed."

God's special blessing to Mary, granted in the opening act of the wonderful drama of Christ's birth, boldly highlights the truth that the Lord gives no grace to those who refuse Him. But as with His unique graciousness to Mary, He grants abundant grace to His chosen ones.

THE DIVINE CHILD

The astonishing appearance of the angel to Mary and the wonderful truth that God had shown great grace to her were just the beginning phases of Gabriel's momentous announcement. Luke 1:31–33 unveils to Mary for the first time what the essence of God's extraordinary work in her life would be: "'And behold, you will conceive in your womb and bring forth a Son, and shall call His name JESUS. He will be great, and will be called the Son of the Highest; and the Lord God will give Him the throne of His father David. And He will reign over the house of Jacob forever, and of His kingdom there will be no end.'"

That is the fourth part of the divine announcement—Mary will be the virgin mother of the divine child, Jesus, the King and Redeemer. If the angel's initial statement that Mary had found favor with God jolted her and caused her much serious reflection, imagine how much more shocking these new words were to her. If it was challenging for Mary to comprehend divine grace extended to her, it must have been even more difficult to grasp that she would conceive God's own Son in her womb.

Mary knew only one way to conceive, and that was to have sexual relations with a man. But she had never had a marital relationship, a fact she attested to with the simple question, "'How can this be, since I do not know a man?'" (v. 34). That was her euphemistic way of affirming that she was still a virgin.

Scripture doesn't tell us what other reactions Mary had to this latest news, but we can reasonably guess her thoughts were something like this: *Well, maybe I'll conceive right after Joseph and I are finally married—after the celebration is over and the marriage is consummated. Surely this news can't be fulfilled any other way.* Humanly speaking, such thoughts would be understandable, because no young woman would think she could have a child without the involvement of a man.

But Mary is not left to wonder and speculate how Gabriel's words will be fulfilled. He provided a most amazing answer to her question—"'The Holy Spirit will come upon you, and the power of the Highest will overshadow you; therefore, also, that Holy One who is to be born will be called the Son of God. Now indeed, Elizabeth your relative has also conceived a son in her old age; and this is now the sixth month for her who was called barren. For with God nothing will be impossible'" (vv. 35–37).

Gabriel was explaining his earlier words (v. 31), which were only a general reference to the virgin birth. However, like another angelic statement in Matthew 1:23, those words were taken from the Greek translation for Isaiah 7:14. Thus, Gabriel's explanation to Mary was the beginning of a fulfillment of that well-known prophecy: "Behold, the virgin shall conceive and bear a Son, and shall call His name Immanuel." His elucidation supports the conclusions we drew in chapter 1 of this study, namely, that Jesus had to be born of a virgin to be the Son of God and a genuine Savior of sinners.

All of Gabriel's words about the divine child, Jesus, constitute a summary of the entire person and work of our Lord and Savior. The summation appears rather simple on the surface, but the complexity of each facet challenges our ability to grasp and appreciate all that the angel said to Mary. It is truly awesome to contemplate Jesus' saving work (in His name), His perfectly righteous life, His title of deity, and His kingly position—all in the same concise overview.

Jesus' Saving Work

First, the angel gives a preliminary indication of the Child's saving mission. Jesus' name itself comes from the Hebrew *Yeshua,* which means "Jehovah saves" (Matt. 1:21). (The God of the Old Testament was a saving God, and His people knew it; 2 Sam. 7:23; Job 19:25; Isa. 44:21–23; 45:21; Hos. 14:2; Joel 2:12–13; Jon. 2:9.) Later in Luke's description of the Incarnation, he reiterates and underscores the point that the Child, Jesus, was the long-awaited Savior: "'For there is born to you this day in the city of David a Savior, who is Christ the Lord'" (2:11); "'For my [Simeon's] eyes have seen Your salvation'" (2:30); "And coming in that instant she [Anna] gave thanks to the Lord, and spoke of Him to all those who looked for redemption in Jerusalem" (2:38). And later in his Gospel, while chronicling Christ's ministry in Perea, Luke conveyed in Jesus' own words the reason He came: "'for the Son of Man has come to seek and to save that which was lost'" (19:10).

Jesus' Perfectly Righteous Life

People use the word *great* in reference to all kinds of things: "Have a great day." "That was a great film." "That would be great." But such frequent uses of this and other similar adjectives tend to water down and trivialize the very notions we try so hard to communicate. Consequently, we often have to struggle with additional adjectives to fully convey what we mean.

That's the impression Luke 1:32 gives with Gabriel's simple statement that Jesus would be great. Certainly there must be a more gripping way to describe the upcoming life of the Messiah. Some commentators would say it's better to translate the Greek word for "great" as "extraordinary." Or it might be better still to substitute the adjective *splendid*. Then additional terms, such as *magnificent, noble, distinguished, powerful*, and *eminent*, come to mind; but they still don't allow us to speak as excitedly as we ought about the life of Jesus. Nevertheless, the Holy Spirit regarded the simple designation "great" as sufficient to describe the extraordinary life of the divine child.

But is Jesus' greatness of life the same as John the Baptist's? After all, Luke earlier reported the angel's words that John would "be great in the sight of the Lord" (1:15). Those words came true; however, John's greatness was a quality God granted to him. In contrast, Jesus' greatness is a quality not merely granted to Him, but inherently possessed by Him.

Christ's greatness is best understood in relation to what the apostle John wrote about Him:

> But although He had done so many signs before them, they did not believe in Him, that the word of Isaiah the prophet might be fulfilled, which he spoke:
> "Lord, who has believed our report?
> And to whom has the arm of the Lord been revealed?"
> Therefore they could not believe, because Isaiah said again:
> "He has blinded their eyes and hardened their hearts,
> Lest they should see with their eyes,
> Lest they should understand with their hearts and turn,
> So that I should heal them."
> These things Isaiah said when he saw His glory and spoke of Him.
> (John 12:37–41)

John's second quotation from the prophet is from Isaiah 6:9–10, when Isaiah witnessed God's glory in the temple and spoke about Him. But when did Isaiah see the glory (or greatness) of Christ? He saw it at the same time he saw the glory of God, because the glory of Christ is the same as the glory of God. The prophet Isaiah knew that one day God was sending the Messiah, His Son, to live a perfect life among His people and to save them from their sins (Isa. 7:14; 9:6–7; 53:4–6). He had a preview of the same glory of Christ that the apostles later witnessed and wrote about (Matt. 17:1–8; John 1:14).

When Gabriel told Mary that Jesus would be great, he meant that Jesus would manifest the very glory of God. That is, people would see the attributes of God displayed through His perfectly righteous life. Whenever you study Luke or the other three Gospels, you see God in every picture of Christ. He talks like God, acts like God, thinks like God, performs miracles that only God could do, teaches truth only God would teach, and responds with the love, goodness, wisdom, and omniscience that only God could possess. And it all begins with the birth of the divine child.

Jesus' Title of Deity

The angel continues in Luke 1:32 his summary of the person and work of Christ: "[He] will be called the Son of the Highest." "Highest" was simply a title for God, clearly indicating that nobody is higher than He is. Mary and other righteous Jews were familiar with that title because it is used throughout the Old Testament. In fact, the Hebrew equivalent of the Greek term used by Luke is one many of us know: *El Elyon*, "God Most High." That title refers to God's sovereignty and the fact that no one is higher, more exalted, or more powerful than He is.

To identify Jesus as the Son of the Highest is to declare that He has the same essence as the Most High God. Hebrews 1:3 says this about Jesus: "who being the brightness of His glory and the express image of His person." Jesus told His disciples, "'He who has seen Me has seen the Father'" (John 14:9). And He boldly asserted to His Jewish opponents, "'I and My Father are one'" (John 10:30).

Gabriel announced, and the New Testament confirms, that Jesus unquestionably was and is worthy of His divine title, because He truly is the Son of God. But His story does not consist only of His amazing birth, extraordinary life, sacrificial death, and miraculous resurrection.

Jesus' Kingly Position

The story of Jesus will wonderfully conclude with His sovereign rule over earth and heaven. "'The Lord God will give Him the throne of His father David. And He will reign over the house of Jacob forever, and of His kingdom there will be no end'" (Luke 1:32–33). The story of redemption will culminate with great precision in the glorious reign of Jesus Christ on David's throne over the nation of Israel, by which He will establish an earthly Kingdom for a thousand years, followed by an eternal Kingdom.

As we saw in our study of the genealogy of Jesus, God sent Him to earth with the proper credentials to rule. He offered His Kingdom to His people, but they spurned it and then rejected and executed Him. However, Christ will return in glory and with omnipotence to establish His Kingdom (Rev. 19:1–21:8).

The Old Testament writers, under the inspiration of the Holy Spirit, foresaw the coming of Christ's Kingdom. For example, David writes, "Yet I have set My King on My holy hill of Zion. I will declare the decree: the Lord has said to Me, 'You are My Son, today I have begotten You. Ask of Me, and I will give You the nations for Your inheritance, and the ends of the earth for Your possession'" (Ps. 2:6–8). In 2 Samuel 7:12–16, God told David he would have a Son who would reign forever. And that Son was not Solomon, but the Messiah, Jesus, as confirmed by the genealogies in Matthew and Luke.

The Bible promises that all believers will be part of Christ's Kingdom. Even though God will take us to heaven through death or the Rapture, He will include us in the millennial Kingdom. Others will be saved during the Tribulation and become members of the Kingdom. Christ will return, kill the unbelieving, and then establish His earthly Kingdom of righteousness, peace, and truth. And once the final rebellion of Satan and his followers is crushed and they're sent to the Lake of Fire, the Lord will establish His eternal Kingdom. The magnificent words of Handel's "Hallelujah Chorus" perfectly describe the conclusion: "He shall reign forever and ever!"

The angel Gabriel's divinely dispatched announcement to the young Mary undoubtedly surpasses in significance any earthly news bulletin that you or I will ever hear. In five clear and concise sentences, Gabriel summarizes all of redemptive history. The proclamation's key elements—such as God's amazing grace to Mary and the attributes of the divine child—ought to remind you daily that the baby once born in Bethlehem now rules your heart and will eventually be your King in the glory of heaven. What monumental truths!

4

Will This News Really Come True?

Chapter Four

❦

Will This News Really Come True?

PERSONAL EMPATHY and identification with other people's experiences and problems is a fascinating thing. It happens regularly and in various ways. You might hear that doctors have told a fellow church member he has lung cancer. Or a good friend could phone you and reveal that her husband has lost his job. On the other hand, a relative could send you a letter or an e-mail message informing you that he has won a free vacation to Europe.

No matter what the example, if the event matches what you've experienced, you naturally want to provide helpful information, understanding, or hope to the other person. And even if you can't identify directly with the other person's experience, you'll probably want to rejoice with him over his good fortune or express your concern about the difficulty he's facing.

The story of Jesus' birth includes a large measure of personal empathy and identification between one of the central characters, Mary, and an important supporting character, Mary's older relative Elizabeth, the mother of John the Baptist. Luke's Gospel reveals the overlap between the extraordinary experiences of those two special women. And it does so in such a way that it's obvious Mary would want to have fellowship with Elizabeth—a fellowship centered on their parallel encounters with the same angel and their desire for reassurance from another believer that God's promise would actually come true.

A CASE OF INCREDIBLE SIMILARITIES

Luke begins his Gospel with the story of two conception miracles, both involving women who at the time could not naturally have children. Elizabeth was in her sixties or seventies, barren, and yet with her elderly husband, Zacharias, she conceived and carried in her womb John the Baptist, the prophesied forerunner of the Messiah. Mary, as we just saw in the previous chapter, was a virgin girl of twelve or thirteen who became pregnant by the power of the Holy Spirit and as a result would give birth to Jesus, the incarnate Son of God. Even though there were differences in their ages and circumstances, both mothers were chosen by God to be human instruments in the two most unusual and significant births in the New Testament. The births marked the great peak in redemptive history, and the Holy Spirit providentially filled the two accounts with incredible, unmistakable similarities.

The two narratives of Luke 1 run as parallel accounts, with the same kind of narrative flow. First, they both begin with an introduction of the child's parents, or parent. Second, both mention specific obstacles to childbearing—Elizabeth's barrenness and Mary's virginity. Third, the angel Gabriel made both announcements, each time to someone living in a small-town, out-of-the-way location. Elizabeth and Zacharias lived in the hill country south of Jerusalem; Mary lived in Nazareth, a small Galilean town north of Jerusalem. Fourth, in both stories there was a fearful first reaction to Gabriel's words and a statement of reassurance from him. Then there was a description of the coming son and, in each case, an objection raised—by Zacharias, unbelief; by Mary, lack of understanding. Last, before Gabriel's respective departures, he guaranteed his announcement would come to pass. So Luke reported on two distinct incidents, separated by several months yet with the same basic elements, all leading to a wonderful convergence.

ELIZABETH ENCOURAGES MARY

The separate encounters of Mary and Elizabeth with Gabriel, which neither woman knew the other had experienced, finally dovetailed shortly after the divine messenger left Mary:

> Now Mary arose in those days and went into the hill country with haste, to a city of Judah, and entered the house of Zacharias and greeted Elizabeth. And it happened, when Elizabeth heard the greeting of Mary, that the babe leaped in her womb; and Elizabeth was filled with the Holy Spirit. Then she spoke out with a loud voice and said, "Blessed are you among women, and blessed is the fruit of your womb! But why is this granted to me, that the mother of my Lord should come to me? For indeed, as soon as the voice of your greeting sounded in my ears, the babe leaped in my womb for joy. Blessed is she who believed, for there will be a fulfillment of those things which were told her from the Lord." (Luke 1:39–45)

The special visit between Mary and Elizabeth poses some obvious questions. What was the main purpose of such a meeting? Why did Mary go with such eagerness and haste to visit Elizabeth? What did it mean when the baby leaped in Elizabeth's womb? And what was the prophecy that Elizabeth gave?

It's easy to deduce why Mary would have wanted to meet with Elizabeth as soon as possible. The news Mary had just heard from Gabriel was startling and mind-boggling. The angel understood how Mary was feeling and graciously gave her a sign that prompted her to quickly embark on the eighty-mile journey to Elizabeth's home: "'Now indeed, Elizabeth your relative has also conceived a son in her old age; and this is now the sixth month for her who was called barren. For with God nothing will be impossible'" (Luke 1:36–37).

Mary believed the angel, but his news was nevertheless beyond normal comprehension. First of all, angels didn't usually speak to mortals, and second, conception miracles just didn't routinely happen. Therefore, it's easy to understand that Mary would welcome anything that might bolster her faith—anything that might underscore the reality that such miracles do occur. After all, the conception that would take place within her body would be completely the result of God's miraculous intervention, without her even knowing when it happened.

Those unique circumstances lead inevitably to further questions, for Mary and for us. How could she withstand the emotional and spiritual strain that went with being the mother of God's Son? And because her pregnancy would not be physically noticeable for a period of time, how could Mary be certain right away that the angel's words had really come to pass? All of those factors compelled Mary to go without delay to visit Elizabeth—the one person who could verify for her that God was able to do a conception miracle.

Mary Receives a Personal Confirmation

The reason the Lord arranged for Mary and Elizabeth's meeting was to confirm the truth of Gabriel's words to Mary. And the first aspect of this confirmation was that it came from Elizabeth, the only one who could provide such personal authentication.

When Mary first heard Elizabeth was pregnant (Luke 1:36), she realized an older woman such as her relative could not be pregnant solely by human means. Mary also knew Elizabeth was far enough along (six months) so that her pregnancy would be clearly evident. Because she planned to leave her elder relative after just three months' visit (1:56–57) and before Elizabeth gave birth, Mary wasted no time in making the trip. She embarked on the four-day journey within days of hearing Gabriel's announcement.

When Mary arrived at Elizabeth's home, she greeted Elizabeth according to the Near Eastern customs of that day. Such greetings were much more lengthy and involved than the simple "Hi, how are you?" that we are accustomed to using today. Exodus 18:7 contains a good illustration of the classic Near Eastern greeting: "So Moses went out to meet his father-in-law, bowed down, and kissed him. And they asked each other about their well-being, and they went into the tent." As verses 8–9 of that chapter go on to describe, those ancient greetings were very special social occasions. The persons involved would embrace, physically display genuine affection for one another, and then engage in a lengthy dialogue about how life was going for each of them. It's safe to assume that's what occurred when Mary first met Elizabeth.

The two cousins definitely had much to talk about. Surely they each would have recounted their recent experiences with the angel Gabriel and marveled at how many similarities the two stories contained. Just listening to Elizabeth and realizing she was indeed pregnant provided a great personal confirmation to Mary. Since God fulfilled what He had promised to Elizabeth, He would also fulfill what He had promised to Mary.

For Mary, it only made sense to tell Elizabeth first about her encounter with the angel a few days earlier. That way Mary's older relative could be a support for her when she told everybody else. Otherwise, if one so young had attempted on her own to share her good news with others, there would have been just a small likelihood that they would accept her amazing story. But Elizabeth was the one person who would have any rationale to accept Mary's testimony. And that's because Elizabeth was a living, personal confirmation that God was doing conception miracles. What a tremendous initial affirmation that must have been for Mary!

Mary Witnesses a Physical Confirmation

During her visit with Elizabeth, Mary also witnessed an amazing physical phenomenon that further confirmed for her that God had placed within her body His only begotten Son. Luke reported this remarkable incident as follows: "And it happened, when Elizabeth heard the greeting of Mary, that the babe leaped in her womb" (1:41).

Such movement of a baby in its mother's womb is certainly not abnormal. In fact, it's probably one of the more enjoyable pleasures of childbearing to feel a baby moving before he or she is born. Almost every parent knows what it's like to place his or her hands on the mother's abdomen and feel the kicking and moving of the infant in the womb. Sensing the baby's movements is thrilling because that action indicates a new person is on the way.

But the movement of Elizabeth's baby was far more significant than that of a normal fetus in a mother's womb. That's because this fetus was a prophet, and not just any prophet, but, according to Scripture, the greatest prophet who ever lived—John the Baptist. His special leap was John's first proclamation, a silent prophecy in his earliest role as the forerunner announcing Christ's coming.

The unborn John was also fulfilling part of the angel's prophecy to his father, Zacharias: "'He will also be filled with the Holy Spirit, even from his mother's womb'" (1:15). But why would God cause such an unusual action? The supreme reason He did so was to achieve something supernatural through John the Baptist while he was still a fetus. God in effect used the unborn John to make an unspoken but enthusiastic prophecy of support for the coming Messiah.

What God did through John was very unusual, but not without precedent. He also prophesied through the unborn Jacob and Esau the future conflict between Israel and the Arabs (Gen. 25:21–23). When it suits His purposes, God can even use the activity inside a mother's womb to preview His plans. We would expect such extraordinary occurrences leading up to the arrival of the Messiah, and John's special prenatal leap was motivated by nothing less than Spirit-filled joy when he sensed the arrival of Mary, the mother of the forthcoming Savior.

The divinely inspired delight John's fetus displayed in approval of the birth of Jesus wonderfully foreshadowed his teaching later on as the forerunner of Christ. "'He who has the bride is the bridegroom; but the friend of the bridegroom, who stands and hears him, rejoices greatly because of the bridegroom's voice. Therefore this joy of mine is fulfilled'" (John 3:29). If there was anything that characterized John the Baptist and his ministry, it was supreme joy. Ultimately, he was joyful because

Christ the Bridegroom had arrived; but his joy originated at the prompting of the Holy Spirit while he was still in Elizabeth's womb.

Would Gabriel's news to Mary really come true? By this point in her visit to Elizabeth, an affirmative answer was coming into clearer focus. First, the testimony of the six-months' pregnant Elizabeth gave Mary personal confirmation that conception miracles can happen. Second, the joyful movement of Elizabeth's son within her womb provided Mary physical confirmation that she would indeed bear the Savior, a fact that would bring joy to many besides John. Next came a divine interpretation through the mouth of Elizabeth of the significance of Mary's extraordinary situation.

Mary Hears a Prophetic Confirmation

During her visit with Elizabeth, Mary received a third confirmation that the angel's recent announcement was true. Luke, the historian and theologian, recorded Elizabeth's prophetic verification this way: "and Elizabeth was filled with the Holy Spirit. Then she spoke out with a loud voice and said, 'Blessed are you among women, and blessed is the fruit of your womb! But why is this granted to me, that the mother of my Lord should come to me? For indeed, as soon as the voice of your greeting sounded in my ears, the babe leaped in my womb for joy. Blessed is she who believed, for there will be a fulfillment of those things which were told her from the Lord'" (1:41–45).

Being filled with the Holy Spirit was often linked to speaking a message from God (2 Sam. 23:2; Luke 1:67; 2:25–28; 2 Pet. 1:21). And when the Spirit filled Elizabeth prior to her crying out, it was simply an example of a familiar scriptural pattern and an indicator that she spoke divine revelation.

When Elizabeth literally shouted in such an unusual manner, she did so in enthusiasm over the incredible truth that Mary was going to bear the Christ. The older cousin also wanted, under the Spirit's direction, to dramatically emphasize the authority of that amazing news. Mary was undoubtedly moved with awe and encouragement as she heard this loud hymn of praise and blessing—one that pronounced blessing in almost every direction.

First, Elizabeth's message pronounced *blessing on Mary:* "'Blessed are you among women.'" This blessing is from a simple Hebrew construction that means, "You're the most blessed of all women."

Elizabeth made such a sweeping statement because in ancient Jewish culture a woman's greatness was based on the greatness of the children she bore (Luke 11:27). Thus Elizabeth was telling Mary that she was most blessed because she was going to give birth to the greatest child ever, the Lord Jesus.

The opening words of Elizabeth's prophecy were actually quite humble because they acknowledged the superiority of her younger relative's privilege. Even though just months earlier God had told Elizabeth and her husband, Zacharias, that her son would be great, she now knew he would not be as great as Mary's son. Elizabeth's son would be the forerunner of the Messiah, but Mary's son would actually be that long-promised Messiah. Therefore, Elizabeth was thrilled to concede that Mary was a greater beneficiary of God's goodness. As a righteous woman, Elizabeth was overjoyed to declare that Mary's calling and privilege was far greater than her own. It was one thing to bear a prophet but another thing altogether to bear the Lord.

Next, Elizabeth had great words of *blessing for the child:* "'Blessed is the fruit of your womb!'" This was a familiar Old Testament phrase that literally means, "Blessed is the child you will bear." According to the unerring prompting of the Holy Spirit, Elizabeth knew Mary's son was going to be the most blessed child ever born. He would receive the full, unmixed, unmitigated blessing of heaven; He would be holy, harmless, undefiled, and perfectly sinless; He would receive all that the Father possesses, including a vast body of redeemed men and women to serve, praise, and glorify Him forever. Without any doubt, Jesus deserved more praise and blessing than any child born before or since.

Third, Elizabeth's prophetic confirmation included a *blessing of her-*

self. In amazement, humility, and awe she wondered aloud how and why it was that the mother of her Lord would have visited her. "The mother of my Lord" was a great statement of prophetic confirmation that the child within Mary's womb was truly the Lord—He was already Elizabeth's Lord. "Lord" is an exalted title of divinity used twenty-five times in Luke 1–2 to refer to God, which further indicates that Elizabeth's statement can only mean that Mary's son was God.

Elizabeth closed her prophetic statement with a general beatitude that was a *blessing on all who believe:* "Blessed is she [anyone] who believed, for there will be a fulfillment of those things which were told her from the Lord" (Luke 1:45). Certainly Elizabeth initially directed this beatitude toward Mary, but its being in the third person demonstrates that the Spirit widened it to include anyone who believes God's revelation. Isn't it true that if we believe God's Word and accept His fulfilled promises, we are blessed?

Mary is a wonderful example of how we should respond to God's message. He did not bless her just because she was privileged to bear the Messiah or because of her elite status in society or because she had a record of good deeds. Instead, God blessed Mary simply because she believed.

Mary is therefore a model of faith. She believed that the angel's divine message to her would be fulfilled. And she settled that faith in her heart and mind by pursuing a sure confirmation of the truth from Elizabeth.

After Mary received Elizabeth's threefold confirmation and all the encouragement that surely accompanied it, she must have rejoiced as she returned home three months later. She apparently did not need to stay for the birth of John the Baptist, and besides, it was time for her to get on with her life because by then she herself was three months' pregnant.

Mary's pattern is how we ought to live our lives. When God speaks to us through His Word, whether it's about the miracle of the Incarnation or any other truth, we must believe He will fulfill His promises. Then we must worship Him and follow up with obedient service. That's the real issue as we consider Mary's visit to Elizabeth and all the other aspects of the story of our Lord's birth.

5

A Humble Birth in Bethlehem

Chapter Five

◆◇◆

A Humble Birth in Bethlehem

THE HISTORICAL SETTING for the world's greatest birth appears in one of the most familiar and best-loved passages in the entire Bible. As Luke raises the curtain on the actual story of the birth of Christ in Luke 2:1–7, he reveals a narrative that is refreshingly simple, clear, and uncluttered:

> And it came to pass in those days that a decree went out from Caesar Augustus that all the world should be registered. This census first took place while Quirinius was governing Syria. So all went to be registered, everyone to his own city.
>
> Joseph also went up from Galilee, out of the city of Nazareth, into Judea, to the city of David, which is called Bethlehem, because he was of the house and lineage of David, to be registered with Mary, his betrothed wife, who was with child. So it was, that while they were there, the days were completed for her to be delivered. And she brought forth her first-born Son, and wrapped Him in swaddling cloths, and laid Him in a manger, because there was no room for them in the inn.

As straightforward and unembellished as Luke's language is, he is dealing with profound and far-reaching issues related to the coming of Jesus Christ.

All scripturally informed Jews knew certain facts about the Messiah who would one day come to earth. They knew He would come from the royal line of David and reign from the throne in Jerusalem over Israel's glorious kingdom. And one thing about Messiah that faithful Jews were certain of was set forth by the prophet Micah, "But you, Bethlehem Ephrathah, though you are little among the thousands of Judah, yet out of you shall come forth to Me the One to be Ruler in Israel, whose goings forth are from of old, from everlasting" (Mic. 5:2).

So it's clear that Jesus, the Messiah, had to be born in Bethlehem, even though Luke 2:1–7 does not quote or even refer to Micah. But the passage does demonstrate how God providentially arranged Christ's birth in Bethlehem in explicit fulfillment of Micah's prophecy.

If events at the dawn of the first century had progressed just ordinarily, Jesus would not have been born in Bethlehem. But God worked in amazing and powerful ways to make the Lord's birth occur precisely at the right time and place, thus verifying His own prophetic Word. God orchestrated Joseph and Mary's visit to Bethlehem—and the circumstances related to it—in such a way that His Son was born exactly according to plan.

THE WORLD SETTING FOR CHRIST'S BIRTH

Caesar Augustus, a prominent emperor during the time Rome occupied Israel, was oblivious to his role in the events leading up to Christ's birth. Yet God providentially directed the emperor's actions precisely in accord with His prophetic timetable. The Lord of course knew when Mary and Joseph had to be in Bethlehem, and He planned for their visit to occur under the authority of a pagan emperor who was utterly ignorant of Scripture.

In keeping with his literary style, Luke used the concise, general expression "in those days" to identify the times prior to Jesus' imminent birth. Implicit in that short phrase is the Jews' general attitude toward conditions then.

They hated the occupation of their land by the Romans—unclean

Gentiles who were outside the covenant. The Jews had no love for Gentiles, and particularly not for the polytheistic Romans. God's people had disdained that brand of idolatry ever since the Babylonian captivity, and now the Romans brought images of their idols (including a deified Caesar) into Israel on patriotic banners and military armor and shields. Particularly distasteful was to see Caesar's idolatrous image on all Roman coinage, which the Jews had to use all the time. But the emperor, simply by virtue of his powerful position, exerted his influence in many other ways.

Augustus was born Gaius Octavius (often called Octavian) in 63 B.C. He was the grandnephew of Julius Caesar, who adopted him as a son and officially declared him the heir to the throne of the Roman Empire.

Octavian didn't immediately ascend to the throne after the assassination of Julius Caesar, but the young man eventually prevailed in a power struggle with Mark Antony and ruled the Empire from 27 B.C. to A.D. 14. During that period, the versatile and able Octavian demonstrated great military, political, and social skills in ending all civil wars and extending Rome's boundaries to the edges of the known world.

Those leadership skills also brought an incredible peace (the so-called Pax Romana, or "peace of Rome") to that vast empire. Such previously unheard-of tranquility allowed for construction of a massive road system that facilitated transportation in every direction and solidified Rome's control. That meant there were no rigid borders between provinces—no border checkpoints, but instead an ease of movement all around the Empire. That reality led to the easy, rapid spread of the gospel and was implicit in Paul's statement to the Galatians, "But when the fullness of the time had come, God sent forth His Son" (Gal. 4:4). Everything on the world scene was perfectly arranged and timed for the arrival of Jesus Christ.

Octavian (who acquired the title *Augustus*, "majestic one, highly honored one," three years before he began his rule) was quite deferential in dealing with his subjects. He granted them limited freedom and autonomy and respected their customs and religions. He even encouraged writers to make literature nobler and passed a measure outlawing adultery; thus, he did have some moral sense.

All in all, Augustus was a fascinating figure who fit amazingly well into God's redemptive plan. He was an unwitting instrument of divine providence and a world leader who helped prepare the way for the first coming of Christ.

Luke refers to one of the most important of those instruments: "a decree went out from Caesar Augustus that all the world should be registered" (2:1). A decree was a common governmental action in those days (Acts 17:7), and it was simply an imperial edict, law, or mandate.

This particular decree said that officials in all parts of the Empire must conduct a registration, or census. ("All the world" was just another way of identifying the Roman Empire.) Rome required such registrations for two reasons. One was to determine which young men were eligible for military service. The other was to assess taxes, which was the case in Luke 2. We know Luke was referring to taxation because Mary and Joseph were involved. They would not have been included in the first type of census because Jews were exempt from Roman military service. In a taxation census, the people registered their names, occupations, property holdings, and family members to the Roman equivalent of the American IRS.

The Jews despised Roman taxation. If they thought the Romans had no right to occupy Israel, the Jews certainly thought the foreigners had no right to exact taxes from them. Their hatred of the Roman tax system manifested itself most intensely in the attitude Jews had toward countrymen who collected taxes for Rome. It's no wonder average Jews like Joseph and Mary likely were not very happy with the decree for a census.

The Jews hated such pagan intrusion into their private lives. But God used the census in Luke 2 to implement His eternal purpose to send His Son. Just as centuries earlier He had used Cyrus's decree to liberate the Jews and return them to reestablish their nation (Ezra 1:1–6; Isa. 44:28–45:4), and just as He had used Nebuchadnezzar for His own purposes (Dan. 3:24–30; 4:28–37), God used Caesar Augustus and his census decree to bring Jesus' parents to Bethlehem at the right time.

History tells us that, due to various delays and difficulties, Caesar's census was not carried out in Palestine until two to four years after it was first announced. But finally, Augustus imposed a strict deadline for compliance, and therefore average Jewish citizens like Joseph and Mary had to hasten their obedience to the edict.

The Romans normally registered people in their current place of residence rather than making them return to their homeland or hometown. But in accord with Jewish custom, Mary and Joseph had to go back to Bethlehem "because he [Joseph] was of the house and lineage of David" (Luke 2:4). From their earliest days as a people, the Jews considered their ancestry important. They divided the Promised Land into tribal areas, and within those areas were towns and villages that belonged to certain families who owned land there. Every fifty years the various lands would revert to the original owners, so genealogies were very important. As we saw in chapter 2 of our study, the Jews kept careful, detailed records of their family histories. That way each man could identify his father's home area and go back there for official obligations such as Caesar Augustus' census. Therefore Jesus' parents were providentially directed to be in Bethlehem at precisely the right time to fulfill Micah 5:2.

THE NATIONAL SETTING FOR CHRIST'S BIRTH

Whenever we think of a national setting in relation to the birth of Christ, the nation of Israel immediately comes to mind. The connection is obvious when you consider Mary and Joseph's journey from Nazareth to Bethlehem. On that arduous trip, they passed through many places that were significant in Old Testament history.

Shiloh, the town where Hannah asked the Lord for a child (1 Sam. 1:9–11), would have greeted them. Then they would have gone through Gilgal, where Hannah's son, Samuel, sat to judge Israel. Jesus' parents also may have passed through the Valley of Baca, of which the psalmist had sung (Ps. 84:6). Their path perhaps wound past Bethel, with all its patriarchal memories, and Ramah, where Jeremiah pictured Rachel weeping for her children (Jer. 31:15). Next, they would have climbed to Gibeon, where Solomon worshiped, and past Mizpah, where Samuel raised his memorial stone called Ebenezer (1 Sam. 7:12). Then they would have gone through the great capital city of Jerusalem, past Mt. Moriah, and across the plateau of Zion on which Jerusalem rests. Finally, in another six miles, Mary and Joseph would have arrived at the town of Bethlehem, the home of Ruth and Boaz (Ruth 4:9–11), the place where Rachel was buried, and, most notable, the town where King David was born.

Luke succinctly summarized that momentous journey this way: "Joseph also went up from Galilee, out of the city of Nazareth, into Judea, to the city of David, which is called Bethlehem" (2:4). That placed the town of Bethlehem and one specific region of Israel, Judea, right at the center of the Nativity story.

To the casual observer, Luke's name for Bethlehem may seem inconsistent with Old Testament designations. That's because in 2 Samuel 5:7 and elsewhere, the hill of Zion *in Jerusalem* is called the city of David. There is, however, no discrepancy between the Old and New Testament names. Zion was the place where David ruled as king—in essence, the city of David within the city of Jerusalem. Luke was simply using the same expression, "city of David," in a different way. Bethlehem is also a city of David; it's not the city where he reigned, but it is the city where he was born.

In fact, the Old Testament clearly affirmed Bethlehem as a city of David long before the birth of Christ. In 1 Samuel 16:1, the Lord commanded Samuel to choose a new king for Israel from among the sons of Jesse the *Bethlehemite,* and the prophet chose his youngest son, David (vv. 11–13). First Samuel 17:12; 2 Samuel 23:14–16, and Psalm 78:70–72 all directly or indirectly connect David with Bethlehem because that's where he was born; that's where his father's house was.

So Joseph, as a descendant of David, had to go to Bethlehem for the census. And, as we saw from the genealogies, Mary was also a descendant of David. Therefore it was fitting that they both went down to Bethlehem to register—it was for both of Jesus' parents the house of their ancestors.

But historians and Bible students have wondered whether Mary really had to accompany Joseph to the registration. We don't know if she had to go along to sign an official document, to declare some properties, or to verify her ancestry. Scripture does not tell us. But we can infer that it must have been very difficult for Mary to explain to her parents that she was pregnant and at the same time insist to them she had not had sexual relations with a man. And others in the community likely would have accused her of lying about her situation.

The resulting shame and embarrassment Mary had to bear would have been troubling. Even after receiving words of encouragement during her visit with Elizabeth, Mary probably would still have endured much scorn and misunderstanding from family and friends in Nazareth.

Therefore, given those difficult conditions, there's no way Joseph would have made the trip to Bethlehem without taking the nine-months'-pregnant Mary with him. Humanly speaking, the trip allowed him to remove her from a difficult social environment and to ensure his presence with her when the baby was born. But, more important, Joseph had God's insight into the real significance of events. He knew Mary was pregnant with the Son of God. He knew the baby would be Jesus, the Messiah, who would save His people from their sins (Matt. 1:20–25).

World and national conditions certainly compelled Jesus' parents to go to Bethlehem. But more crucial than those factors, they had to travel there to fulfill the clear statement of the prophet Micah. Mary and Joseph had to be in Bethlehem so that it indeed would be the birthplace of a special ruler: "yet out of you shall come forth to Me the One to be Ruler in Israel" (Mic. 5:2). This was a clear reference to the Messiah. It couldn't have referred to David, because he was born three hundred years prior to this prophecy. Furthermore, the prophet's words "whose goings forth are from of old, from everlasting" could refer only to deity. Messiah is an eternal being, a ruler to be born in Bethlehem, yet One who has been alive forever. Every believing Jew who looked forward to the coming of the true Messiah knew that Micah's prophecy pointed unmistakably to Him.

Thus Luke, without actually mentioning Micah 5:2, relates the story of Jesus' birth to the nation of Israel and its people, the Jews. He knew

God had given the Old Testament Scripture to the Jews; and that Scripture, through the words of Micah 5:2, was explicit about the location of Christ's birth—Bethlehem.

THE PERSONAL SETTING FOR CHRIST'S BIRTH

The world and national settings attendant to the birth of Christ are both crucial to helping us understand how God providentially brought about that glorious event within the context of human history. But the much-loved charm of the Incarnation story derives from a third setting—the personal one.

Luke continues his simple account with this general phrase, "So it was, that while they were there" (2:6). We know that Joseph and Mary were in Bethlehem, but it's not initially clear where in the village they were or exactly how long they had been there. They had probably been there at least three days, perhaps even a week, because the writer then says, "the days were completed for her to be delivered."

But we don't have to wonder for long where the young couple was when Jesus was born: "there was no room for them in the inn" (v. 7). These simple words have always excited profound imagination in the minds of readers. Practically speaking, during their stay in Bethlehem, Mary and Joseph were among the homeless.

That does not mean they were completely outside in the cold, but simply that they had no comfortable accommodations. Mary and Joseph were not staying in some sort of three-story hotel, or even a low-budget annex to such a facility. The Greek word for "inn" in verse 7 is not the usual term for inn. Instead, Luke used a word that denoted a shelter or place of lodging for guests. It was not an actual inn operated for the feeding and housing of guests. Instead, it was more like the sleeping section of a public shelter or campground.

Typically, such shelters had four sides and two levels, with the top part being like the loft in a barn. One section of the shelter may have had crude doors to close it off if desired. The entire structure would have been quite primitive, the kind of place where travelers could spend one or more nights in the loft area and keep their animals down in the center area, safe from theft. Their goods could be stored in the center as well.

Because of the Roman decree, Bethlehem would have been a crowded town with all the best rooms already taken. Therefore Mary and Joseph wound up staying with the animals in one of the public shelters. For an undetermined number of days, the young couple likely would have huddled on the shelter's ground floor—among the camels, donkeys, and their feed troughs—because the other part of the shelter ("the inn") was already filled. During that time they would have used their own robes and maybe an extra blanket to shield themselves from the cold winds. We don't know the details of how long they stayed in the shelter, whether they registered before the birth of the baby, or whether they were waiting for the birth before they registered. But we do know they made sure they stayed in Bethlehem until after Mary gave birth to Jesus.

With all the circumstances perfectly arranged, the most important of all births in human history finally occurred. But Luke reports the birth of our Lord and Savior with amazingly few details and merely says, "she brought forth her firstborn Son" (2:7). Because the Gospel text gives us no descriptive details, I think it's safe to engage in a little sanctified imagination concerning what happened that night.

Imagine Joseph being anxious with curiosity, wondering what his Son, who would be the God-Man, might actually be like. He no doubt held Mary's hand throughout her labor, perhaps soothing her forehead with a cool cloth. Like any good husband, Joseph surely would have spoken many words of sweet comfort to his young wife while she endured labor pains. After all, the couple was in a dark, drab place that offered no birthing amenities such as the help of doctors and nurses or even the presence of her mother. Any normal young mother in those days would want her mother present, but Mary had the assistance and reassurance of only a teenaged husband.

We can also imagine that after a certain period of labor, Mary would have pushed one final time to bring forth her child. In the fullness of time God sent forth His Son, born of a woman. At that very moment, the God of eternity stepped into earthbound time and space. As the apostle John wrote later, "the Word became flesh and dwelt among us" (John 1:14). The omnipotent, omnipresent Lord of the universe appeared as a baby, crying the cry of life, probably weighing less than ten pounds and measuring fewer than twenty-four inches in length. The little life would have rested immediately in the arms of young Joseph, who, along with Mary, probably did not comprehend right away the magnitude of what was going on—even though an angel had earlier informed both of them about this extraordinary birth.

Luke, however, is careful to tell us something of the significance of the baby Jesus when he identifies Him as Mary's "firstborn Son." Jesus was not the only son Mary ever had—He was not her *monogenes*, "only begotten," as He was the Father's. But He was the *prototokon*, "firstborn." That's important because it's consistent with Mary's virginity, and it means Jesus had the primary right to the family inheritance. It was a privilege the Old Testament called the all-important right of primogenitor. Neither Joseph nor Mary, as working-class people, had wealthy estates. But as two descendants of King David, they passed on to Jesus the right to rule from David's throne, the throne of Christ's people, Israel.

Luke 2:7 contains other details that are simple and familiar, yet nonetheless fascinating. For instance, have you ever wondered why it says Mary "wrapped Him in swaddling cloths"? *Swaddling* is an Old English word that describes wrapping with cloth. The ancient custom was to wrap the arms, legs, and body of the baby with long strips of cloth to provide warmth and security. Parents in those days also believed that wrapping the child helped his or her bones to grow straight.

Luke's point in mentioning the wrapping cloths, however, is that Mary treated Jesus the way any mother would treat a normal newborn. Physically, He looked like any other child, and his parents treated Him as such. God did not provide Him with royal robes or other fancy clothing, but simply directed Mary and Joseph to welcome Him as they would any other beloved child.

Then there's the familiar phrase "and laid Him in a manger." A more literal translation of the Greek word for "manger" is "feeding trough." From that we can further deduce that Joseph and Mary were staying in the section of the shelter that accommodated travelers' animals. In the ancient Near East, a traveling salesman had a beast of burden to carry his merchandise. Similarly, a traveling family used a pack animal to carry the women and children. As we described earlier, Jesus' parents were huddled in a section of the shelter next to the animals, and they conveniently made His first bed a feeding trough.

When Christ entered the world, He came to a place that had some of the smelliest, filthiest, and most uncomfortable conditions. But that is part of the wonder of divine grace, isn't it? When the Son of God came down from heaven, He came all the way down. He did not hang on to His equality with God; rather, He set it aside for a time and completely humbled Himself (Phil. 2:5–8).

Jesus did not merely humble Himself and agree to be born in a smelly stable, but He humbled Himself as a substitute for wretched sinners and bore the stench of their guilt in His own body on the Cross. He came down to the common people to bring them His glorious salvation. The picture of the infant Son of God tolerating a stable's dirt and foul odors is a fitting metaphor for the later scene of the Savior bearing the stench of sin as He died at Calvary. What an amazing picture!

And, to a certain extent, the site of Christ's birth was also a lonely picture, because of the obscurity of it all. But that situation didn't last long. As we'll see in the next chapter, a group of angels appeared to some nearby shepherds and in glorious fashion announced to them the Son of God's first advent.

6

The Heavenly Announcement of Jesus' Birth

Chapter Six

⟨◈⟩

The Heavenly Announcement of Jesus' Birth

HROUGHOUT HISTORY, people have continually looked for deliverers, majestic leaders they could hail as great saviors from all their troubles. It was no different at the time just prior to Jesus' birth. The Romans hoped for some kind of world savior, and archaeological evidence shows that they actually gave Caesar Augustus the title "Savior of the World." But while Caesar Augustus was in Rome feeling the pride and prestige of that status, the true Savior of the world was born in obscurity in Bethlehem of Judea.

Jesus Christ was born in a small, little-known town, and at first no one knew about it. None of the residents of Bethlehem or its many visitors knew. The officials in Rome and the inhabitants of Jerusalem had no idea what had occurred. For anyone who was near enough to hear it, Jesus' infant cry was just the cry of another baby. The event was so far from center stage that no earthly authority was even aware enough to make a community announcement. However, Mary and Joseph knew that an extraordinary, unprecedented birth had transpired, and others would soon realize it as well.

All heaven broke loose when angels appeared and started praising God to a small and most unlikely audience. Some anonymous shepherds were about to hear news of one of the greatest events in the saga of God's eternal plan:

Now there were in the same country shepherds living out in the fields, keeping watch over their flock by night. And behold, an angel of the Lord stood before them, and the glory of the Lord shone around them, and they were greatly afraid. Then the angel said to them, "Do not be afraid, for behold, I bring you good tidings of great joy which will be to all people. For there is born to you this day in the city of David a Savior, who is Christ the Lord. And this will be the sign to you: You will find the Babe wrapped in swaddling cloths, lying in a manger."

And suddenly there was with the angel a multitude of the heavenly host praising God and saying:

"Glory to God in the highest,
And on earth peace, goodwill toward men!" (Luke 2:8–14)

THE PROCLAMATION OF THE GOOD NEWS

The supernatural announcement that cold night near Bethlehem was truly the high point of redemptive history to that time. The angels' message was nothing less than the good news—the gospel proclaimed with great joy. God's messengers could not wait to proclaim to the shepherds and the world that at last the Savior was here, the One who would deliver His people from the curse of sin, death, and hell, and who would bring them the blessings of His kingdom and the glories of eternity in heaven.

The Unlikeliness of the Shepherds

If you were a modern public relations agent in charge of getting out the news of Christ's birth, the last group you would have picked to be the first to inform would have been a small band of shepherds. Instead, you likely would have targeted the influencers, the real movers and shakers.

You might have considered telling the high priest first, because he was the religious leader of the nation. Or you might have weighed the advantages of going first to the chief priest and scribes, the leading teachers in Israel. On the other hand, you might have thought it smart to go first to the Sanhedrin, the body of seventy elders that was the theocratic leadership of Israel. Or you might have insisted on informing the Pharisees first. After all, they were the religious fundamentalists who were very strict about Old Testament prophecies and looked forward to the Messiah's arrival. You might even have wanted to send an official press release to Caesar Augustus to make sure he knew the true Savior had recently come into the world.

But none of those alternatives was God's option for revealing the news of Christ's birth. Instead, He first took the special message to one of the unlikeliest classes of people imaginable, an obscure group of shepherds. They were not so unlikely, however, if you consider Isaiah's prophecy about Messiah's mission: "The Spirit of the Lord God is upon Me, because the Lord has anointed Me to preach good tidings to the poor; He has sent Me to heal the brokenhearted, to proclaim liberty to the captives, and the opening of the prison to those who are bound" (61:1; Matt. 11:5; Luke 4:18). Thus when Jesus came, He did not go first of all to the people of prestige, influence, and clout. He came first to the poor and lowly, the meek and afflicted—anyone who was outcast— and the shepherds fit that category.

They were the kind of people for whom God always has a special place. After she learned she would be the mother of Christ, Mary praised God for honoring the humble: "'He has put down the mighty from their thrones, and exalted the lowly'" (Luke 1:52). And the apostle Paul teaches us that the lowly were and are the primary objectives of God's saving plan: "For you see your calling, brethren, that not many wise according to the flesh, not many mighty, not many noble, are called. But God has chosen the foolish things of the world to put to shame the wise, and God has chosen the weak things of the world to put to shame the things which are mighty; and the base things of the world and the things which are despised God has chosen, and the things which are not, to bring to nothing the things that are, that no flesh should glory in His presence" (1 Cor. 1:26–29). The Lord's preference for the lowly started at the very beginning of the Gospels, reflected in the angels' bringing the good news of the Savior's birth to shepherds, some of the commonest and most unappreciated of laborers in Jewish society.

The point is not that shepherding was somehow an inherently illegitimate occupation. To realize this, we need only to remember a few prominent biblical examples of shepherds. Abraham was a herdsman who owned much livestock, including sheep. Moses worked for a number of years in Midian as a shepherd for his father-in-law. And a thousand years before Jesus was born, David watched sheep in fields near Bethlehem.

So shepherding was not a shameful profession, just a lowly one that included many menial tasks. Shepherds were basically an insignificant class of workers, poorly educated and poorly paid. In fact, because it did not require much skill, people often gave the task of shepherding to children.

Shepherds were also the lowest people on the Jewish social ladder because they had to care for sheep seven days a week. That work schedule meant they could not observe the Sabbath the way Mosaic Law dictated. Neither could shepherds keep the myriad fastidious, man-made regulations the Pharisees had foisted on top of the Law. Such legalism confounded most of the common Jews, and certainly the shepherds couldn't abide by all of those rules either. Therefore, to one degree or another, people viewed shepherds as outcasts because they violated religious law.

In fact, as the strict legalism of the Pharisees grew and permeated more and more of Jewish society, shepherds became more despised than ever. Soon they were considered unreliable, dishonest, unsavory characters, guilty of sheep stealing and many other illegal activities.

Such an unfavorable portrait of shepherds in Bible times might well be completely contrary to the Sunday school teaching you received. There the lessons usually portrayed shepherds as some kind of special people; but they were actually the least special of any class. Nonetheless, God used the shepherds' social and religious status to perfectly implement His plan for announcing the Savior's arrival.

The Lord's favor toward the shepherds aligned well with His historic disdain for the religious establishment's hypocritical attempt to be right with Him through their own efforts. Thus the Lord effectively underscored the superiority of His grace over man's works when He announced Messiah's birth to a group of lowly shepherds. During His ministry, Jesus further demonstrated His love and acceptance for the humble when He gladly called Himself the Good Shepherd.

All of this is a wonderful metaphor of God's salvation sovereignly extended to the undeserving sinner. The apostle Paul understood this truth when he wrote to Timothy "that Christ Jesus came into the world to save sinners, of whom I am chief" (1 Tim. 1:15). The lower the sinner, the greater is God's glory when He saves him.

God's Glory Revealed to the Shepherds

The angel revealed the greatness of God's glory in a spectacular way to the shepherds in Luke 2:9: "an angel of the Lord stood before them, and the glory of the Lord shone around them, and they were greatly afraid." That occurred during the same twenty-four-hour period in which Jesus was born in nearby Bethlehem; and it was right in the midst of the shepherds' usual nighttime sequence of watching the sheep, taking turns sleeping, telling stories, and perhaps playing their flutes.

We can hardly even imagine what startled, frightened feelings the shepherds had when suddenly, with no warning whatsoever, the highest of all created beings showed up in blazing glory. In fact, it's difficult to describe the dramatic significance of that moment. Luke says, "the glory of the Lord shone around them," an expression we often take for granted but which denotes one of the high points in all of history.

The full impact of Luke's portrayal hits home if you just consider what the glory of the Lord is. Simply defined, it is the presence of God revealed in light. We know that God does not have a physical body, but exists as the invisible Spirit. But when He has revealed Himself to human beings, He has done so with an incomprehensible, brilliant manifestation of pure light. That light is so powerful that if God revealed it fully to mortals, they would be incinerated at once. Here's how the Lord dealt with Moses when he wanted to see the divine glory: "But He said, 'You cannot see My face; for no man shall see Me, and live.' And the LORD said, 'Here is a place by Me, and you shall stand on the rock. So it shall be, while My glory passes by, that I will put you in the cleft of the rock, and I will cover you with My hand while I pass by. Then I will take away My hand, and you shall see My back; but My face shall not be seen'" (Exod. 33:20–23).

The glory of God appeared at other times to His people in the Old Testament. When Moses and the people finished building and arranging the Tabernacle according to God's instructions, "Then the cloud covered the tabernacle of meeting, and the glory of the LORD filled the tabernacle. And Moses was not able to enter the tabernacle of meeting, because the cloud rested above it, and the glory of the LORD filled the tabernacle" (Exod. 40:34–35). It was a monumental episode when the Lord blessed the establishment of the true place of worship. The people finally had an official place to offer sacrifices for sin and receive access to God, and that's why He gave His approval by sending the dazzling cloud of His Shekhinah glory.

Centuries later, when Israel completed Solomon's Temple, the same phenomenon occurred (1 Kings 8:10–11). However, in a relatively short time, the people turned away from God and He responded by withdrawing His glory (see Ezek. 8–10, especially 10:18–19). What a sad moment that had to be for the prophet Ezekiel as he witnessed the divine glory departing.

But God's glory returned the night the angels confronted the shepherds near Bethlehem. This signifies the tremendous importance of that extraordinary night—the presence of God returned to earth, not in a tent or a building as before, but in human flesh in the person of the Messiah.

The Shepherds' Initial Reaction

So the shepherds, the lowliest class of people, witnessed the momentous return to earth of God's glory. And understandably, they did so initially with a great deal of fright. They were absolutely awestruck, over-whelmed, and certainly intimidated by what they were seeing. But there's nothing new about that reaction. In similar circumstances, other figures in the history of God's program responded the same way.

For example, when the prophet Isaiah saw God in a vision, he was so terrified that he pronounced a curse on himself and expected to die immediately (Isa. 6:5). When Ezekiel saw a similar vision of God's glory, he fell on his face in a coma (Ezek. 1:28). When the angel Gabriel came to Zacharias and Mary, respectively, each of them was very fearful (Luke 1:12, 29). When Peter, James, and John saw Christ's glory on the Mount of Transfiguration, they fell down on their faces in terror (Matt. 17:6–7). And at the end of the New Testament, when the apostle John saw the Shekhinah glory of the ascended Christ, he passed out from fear (Rev. 1:17).

If those were the responses of great men and women of faith when they witnessed the glory of God, how could we expect some common, unlearned shepherds to behave any differently or more bravely when the angel suddenly appeared to them? They were ordinary men, probably without any interesting life experiences, who certainly did not expect to witness anything as phenomenal as they did the night of Jesus' birth. But the fact that they did establishes the magnitude of what was going on. Not just any baby was born in nearby Bethlehem. God's own Son, the Savior of sinners, had just come into the world, and the Father was announcing the news in an extraordinary fashion through heavenly messengers.

But if the shepherds' reaction upon suddenly seeing an angel was normal, was it necessary? Scripture on many occasions says sinful people ought to fear God's wrath if their sins are not forgiven. However, the angel in this instance told the shepherds, "'Do not be afraid'" (Luke 2:10). Therefore, this is a sure indicator that the shepherds were devout men whose sins were forgiven. As such, they understood the need for men and women to fear and reverence God (Deut. 10:12–13; Ps. 111:10). But this was not a time when the shepherds should have been afraid of God's impending judgment.

Often when the phrase "Do not be afraid" is used in Scripture it means that, in the particular context, one truly does not need to fear because God's grace has been revealed (Gen. 15:1; Exod. 14:13; Deut. 31:6; Isa. 43:1; Matt. 28:5; Luke 1:13, 30; 5:10; Rev. 1:17). And so it was for the shepherds the night the angel came to them. We need not be afraid in God's presence when He heralds His gracious purpose or announces good news.

That is exactly what the angel announced to the shepherds. It was not dread news of punishment or judgment, but very good news that would elicit great joy in the hearts of those who looked for the Messiah. The phrase "I bring you good tidings" (Luke 2:10) is from the Greek verb *euangelizo,* from which we get the transliterated English word *evangelize.* Of course, that's the familiar term that literally means to tell people the good news. The noun form of the word occurs frequently in the New Testament and is synonymous with the essential message of Christianity, the gospel.

The angel proclaimed the good news of a merciful God who had just sent a Savior who would die on the Cross and forgive forever the sins of all who believe. And the angel knew that such good news ought to produce "great joy" (literally, "laughter, hilarity"), the utter opposite of debilitating fearfulness. Anyone who genuinely receives the good news of the gospel cannot do so without rejoicing tremendously. In essence, the shepherds went from sheer terror to supreme glee when they heard the supernatural announcement. News of the gospel produces the highest joy for repentant sinners and ought to overshadow all other news in importance.

THE PERVASIVENESS OF THE GOOD NEWS

Just how widespread is this joyous good news? Is it for only the favored few or restricted to just the educated elite? We know that's not true if the angel appeared to the lowly shepherds and confirmed the pervasiveness of the gospel by telling those ordinary men that it " 'will be to all people. For there is born to you this day in the city of David, a Savior who is Christ the Lord' " (vv. 10–11).

"All people" refers primarily to the people of Israel, because salvation was first promised to God's people, the Jews. That night God was delivering and ratifying the New Covenant in fulfillment of the Abrahamic and Davidic promises, and He knew the shepherds would have a general understanding of the covenant concept that God was the Redeemer of Israel.

But the expression "all people" encompasses far more than just the nation of Israel. Eight days later, the aged Simeon uttered these prophetic words as he held the baby Jesus in the Temple: "'For my eyes have seen Your salvation which You have prepared before the face of all peoples, a light to bring revelation to the Gentiles, and the glory of Your people Israel'" (Luke 2:30–32). That statement expands the angel's words and makes "all people" truly mean all people without distinction, namely, the Gentiles throughout the world. Isaiah indicated the same truth centuries earlier: "Arise, shine; for your light has come! And the glory of the LORD [Messiah] is risen upon you. For behold, the darkness shall cover the earth, and deep darkness the people; but the LORD will arise over you, and His glory will be seen upon you. The Gentiles shall come to your light" (Isa. 60:1–3; 9:2; 42:6; 49:6–9; 61:1). The prophet was describing the arrival and spread of the gospel. From the beginning of God's plan, the gospel of Christ went to Israel first and then through Israel to all the nations.

The pervasiveness of the gospel, however, also includes an individual aspect. The angel told the shepherds that Christ the Savior had been born "to you." He could have said it this way: "The Savior has been born, and His salvation will be sufficient for everyone, and He will save individuals like you who repent and by faith embrace His work on the Cross." The gospel is for the humblest and lowliest, the most uneducated and unskilled, the most despised, even the worst of sinners. The Son of God, the One born as a baby that special night, came as the Savior for the shepherds and everyone who believes.

THE PERSON OF THE GOOD NEWS

Any kind of significant good news will always involve people, but those who are the most important in the story will not be the same ones every time. Sometimes the one who discloses the news is the key player. In other instances, the people directly affected by the news are the most important. And sometimes the one who is the author of the news is the most noteworthy. That third scenario definitely applied to the announcement of the good news of salvation.

The angel hastened to direct the shepherds' attention to the One bringing salvation, the person of the good news: "'For there is born to ~~~ this day in the city of David a Savior who is Christ the Lord'" (Luke 2:11). The angel didn't use the Child's earthly name, Jesus, as he did when he announced His birth to Joseph (Matt. 1:21). Instead, he identified the One born that night by His twofold heavenly title, "Christ the Lord."

Jesus Is the Christ

Christ is quite an exalted title for a baby born into such humble circumstances as Jesus was. He wore no gold crown and had no halo over His head to identify Him as someone special. There were no outwardly distinctive marks of His deity, His sovereignty, or His Messiahship. As we noted before, in physical appearance Jesus was simply like any other baby. Therefore it's all the more remarkable that Jesus should bear the title "Christ."

In both the Greek translation of the Old Testament and the Greek New Testament, the title *Christos* ("Christ") means "the anointed one." That usage in reference to the future Savior occurs as early as Daniel 9:25–26 (where *Christos* is simply the equivalent of the Hebrew *Messiah*). Whenever the term was used in biblical times, it signified that an ultimate authority was anointing someone and placing him in a very high office.

In Jesus' case, the ultimate authority who anointed Him was His Father. And God did so first of all because Jesus is the King. Anointing was the symbolic way kings were recognized and set apart above their subjects. Therefore, Jesus' being called the Christ indicates that He is

God's anointed King. He is the eternal King of kings who will sit on David's throne and reign over His Kingdom forever. Jesus, at the very end of His earthly ministry, confirmed the truth of His Kingship in this exchange with Pontius Pilate: "Pilate therefore said to Him, 'Are You a king then?' Jesus answered, 'You say rightly that I am a king. For this cause I was born, and for this cause I have come into the world, that I should bear witness to the truth'" (John 18:37).

God also anointed Jesus as our great High Priest (which, as with kings, paralleled an actual ancient practice, that of anointing priests and high priests). "For there is one God and one Mediator between God and men, the Man Christ Jesus" (1 Tim. 2:5). Thus Jesus is the ultimate, glorious High Priest, the great Intercessor who alone can truly take sinners into the presence of a holy God (Heb. 9:11–15). His atoning death literally severed the veil that previously separated men and women from God.

Finally, God anointed Jesus to be our Great Prophet. It was also standard practice in the Old Testament era to anoint prophets because they were thereby set apart as God's spokesmen. But now Jesus would be God's ultimate spokesman, the greatest preacher who ever lived: "God, who at various times and in various ways spoke in time past to the fathers by the prophets, has in these last days spoken to us by His Son, whom He has appointed heir of all things" (Heb. 1:1–2).

It remains ever amazing that the angel was identifying the average-looking baby in the Bethlehem travelers' shelter as the greatest King, Priest, and Prophet the world would ever know. Therefore Christ's coming as a lowly infant is even more humanly incomprehensible because from before the foundation of the world He was already the Father's anointed Ruler, Intercessor, and Spokesman. In gracious love and mercy, God chose Him to be our Messiah, the Christ.

Jesus Is the Lord

The angel also told the shepherds that momentous night that the One born in Bethlehem is the Lord. That title of honor may at first seem insignificant because in ordinary usage it simply denotes a highly esteemed benefactor, patron, or authoritative leader. Over the centuries, for example, the aristocratic class in England has had many men with the title "lord," and that's been a tradition in some other European countries as well.

The New Testament does affirm the use of *lord* as a legitimate designation for certain people: "as Sarah obeyed Abraham, calling him lord" (1 Peter 3:6). The apostle Peter recognizes that submissive wives will view their husbands as those who have a degree of authority over them. So we can use the term to speak of a proper type of human authority.

However, when the angel used "Lord" in his declaration to the shepherds, he was not using a mere human designation. Instead, he was using a divine designation and claiming that the Child in Bethlehem is God. To say that Jesus is Lord is to say that He is first and foremost God. In fact, it is the most fundamental and essential confession of the Christian faith. It is unequivocal that if any person desires to be saved, he must make the heartfelt and vocal confession that Jesus is Lord (Rom. 10:9).

In addition to that, the expression "Jesus is Lord" implies all the sovereignty and authority associated with One who is God. For "Lord" in Luke 2:11, the angel used the Greek word *kurios,* which expresses an authority that is valid and lawful. The ultimate lawful authority in the universe, of course, is God. So the angel was saying Jesus is lawfully Lord because of who He is, the Son of God. The Greek translators of the Old Testament and the writers of the New Testament used *kurios* so often to refer to God that it became synonymous for the name of God. So when the angel declared Jesus to be Lord, he was declaring Him to be the true God, the One who possesses all authority and sovereignty.

The heavenly messenger was certain of the identity of the baby in the manger. The Child was none other than the person of the good news— the Christ who was Prophet, Priest, and King, and the Lord who was God in human flesh. That identity was perfectly in line with Isaiah's words centuries earlier, "For unto us a Child is born, unto us a Son is given; and the government will be upon His shoulder. And His name will be called Wonderful, Counselor, Mighty God, Everlasting Father, Prince of Peace" (Isa. 9:6).

THE PURPOSE OF THE GOOD NEWS

Just when we thought Luke's narrative of Jesus' birth could not get any more exciting, the divinely inspired historian takes us to new dramatic heights. As the good news unfolds, it has a purpose: "And suddenly there was with the angel a multitude of the heavenly host praising God and saying: 'Glory to God in the highest, and on earth peace, goodwill toward men!'" (Luke 2:13–14).

Those eloquent, well-known verses bring us to the highest point of truth and action in Luke's account, and indeed in all of Scripture. They describe the highest, most sublime response to truth that can occur in the created universe. The angels, as supernatural beings created by God, were glorifying Him, which is the ultimate purpose of the gospel.

But many Christians might say, "I thought the purpose of the good news was to save sinners." And they would be right; that is a vital purpose of the gospel. However, the gospel's ultimate purpose is to save sinners so they can join the angels in glorifying God. The final reason for anything believers do is to glorify God.

Besides the basic announcement of Christ's birth, the angel had to proclaim to the shepherds the awesome purpose of such good news— our giving glory to God. And in keeping with the extraordinary nature of that night, he revealed the additional message in dramatic fashion. As if it were not incredible enough that one angel had moments before appeared to them, many angels glorifying God abruptly flashed into view before the shepherds: "suddenly there was with the angel a multitude of the heavenly host praising God" (Luke 2:13).

We don't know precisely how many angels constituted the heavenly host, or army, but "multitude" is the translation of the Greek that means "ten thousand." Years later, the apostle John saw "ten thousand times ten thousand, and thousand of thousands" of angels (Rev. 5:11; 1 Kings

22:19), so it's safe to say that there could have been at least one hundred million. Obviously, not every single angel in heaven appeared to the shepherds, but they did see and hear a very large, representative group. The point is that a vast array of angels—perhaps more than anyone in redemptive history had ever seen—suddenly joined the single angel and did what God's messengers always do, praise and glorify Him.

But why were they praising and glorifying God? On that most unusual of nights, the angels praised Him because Jesus the Savior was born. God had informed them long ago of His plan of salvation. They understood humanity's fall into sin and that Jesus Christ, the majestic second member of the Trinity, would lay aside His riches, come to earth in humility for undeserving sinners, live a perfectly righteous life, and finally die on the cross to bear the curse and punishment of their sins. They understood the true significance of Christ's birth and were praising God because at last they saw the beginning of the final phase of His redemptive plan.

The shepherds heard the angelic host's entire praise summarized in one magnificent sentence: "'Glory to God in the highest, and on earth peace, goodwill toward men!'" (Luke 2:14). This is a declaration of the profoundest truth, yet over the years people have greatly misunderstood and underappreciated the last two phrases of it.

First, "on earth peace" does not refer to peace of mind, rest for the weary, or absence of wars. The angels meant peace with God that results from genuine salvation. Because His Son has brought reconciliation, we no longer need to be God's enemies. The angels were praising the Father, giving Him glory in heaven, because He sent salvation down to earth in the person of Jesus Christ.

The second phrase, "goodwill toward men," also deserves an accurate understanding. For decades people have used this phrase out of context and trivialized it to mean pleasant sentiments at Christmas or kind words and deeds extended to others. Those thoughts are obviously not what the angels had in mind. But even if we seek to know the actual intent of those very recognizable words, we can go astray if we're not careful.

Both the New King James Version, "goodwill toward men" (which is identical to the King James Version), and the New American Standard Bible, "with whom He is pleased," sound as though God is going to grant spiritual peace to those who deserve it or earn it. But an alternate reading makes the meaning more clear: "Peace among men of His good pleasure." Men and women do not earn God's peace, but He gives it to them because He is pleased to do so.

There are some to whom God sovereignly gives the peace of His salvation. The multitude of angels was not rejoicing for what people had done or would do to merit salvation. Rather, the heavenly host was glorifying God because, though none can merit salvation, God is delighted to give it to a vast number of sinners solely by His own good pleasure.

If you have received the gift of salvation, you have God's good pleasure. And He deserves all the credit and all the glory for that gracious reality. In fact, what occurred on that evening near Bethlehem was a mere preview and foretaste of the kind of endless praise we will render once we are in heaven (Rev. 5:11–14).

If you know God is pleased with you, you will thank Him for the pervasiveness of the gospel—that you were privileged to hear it and believe it. And you will respond quickly and obediently to do His will throughout your life. That was the shepherds' response, as chapter 7 will describe.

7

The Testimony of Shepherds

Chapter Seven

❧

The Testimony of Shepherds

HOW DO YOU RESPOND to an especially intense, exciting, and memorable event or activity? What do you feel when confronted suddenly with unexpected news or a major surprise? There is no one answer, obviously. It depends on what you have just seen, heard, or experienced.

A particularly engaging film can evoke happy emotions or provoke sad ones. Seeing a spectacular fireworks presentation or hearing a stirring concert can result in great exhilaration. Watching an exciting, tense ball game between excellent, evenly matched teams can leave you emotionally drained no matter which team won.

On a more serious note, if you're the first eyewitness to a spectacular fire, a horrific traffic accident, or a major plane crash, your first impulse—unless you are in a position to rescue some of the victims—is to notify the authorities immediately. Later, you likely will have to give an official statement to investigators about what you saw.

All those possible scenarios pale into insignificance, almost triviality, when compared to what the little group of shepherds witnessed the night Christ was born. But there is one common thread—the need and desire to talk about the experience, to tell others what was seen and heard. However, it is still hard for us to fully identify with the shepherds' extraordinary situation two thousand years ago.

With the exception of a few broadly similar Old Testament events and several New Testament incidents that were yet future, what the shepherds saw in the skies near Bethlehem the night of our Savior's birth was unprecedented in human experience. An angel, accompanied by a countless multitude of other heavenly messengers, suddenly and unforgettably intervened in the shepherds' mundane, working-class existence with a news bulletin to end all news bulletins. The long-awaited Christ, the Savior of the world, God in human flesh, had just been born in a shelter in nearby Bethlehem. It was all far beyond anything previously imaginable to those lowly men whom society so disregarded.

It may be hard to place ourselves into the shepherds' situation, but they responded to what they saw and heard much the same way as we would respond to far more ordinary events—they had to find out more, and they had to tell others. Even more to the point, the shepherds' response serves as a good illustration of how people respond in a saving manner to the gospel.

THE SHEPHERDS' PLAN OF ACTION

In his simple, straightforward style, Luke chronicles the shepherds' immediate response to their awesome encounter with the angelic visitors:

> So it was, when the angels had gone away from them into heaven, that the shepherds said to one another, "Let us now go to Bethlehem and see this thing that has come to pass, which the Lord has made known to us." And they came with haste and found Mary and Joseph, and the Babe lying in a manger. Now when they had seen Him, they made widely known the saying which was told them concerning this Child. And all those who heard it marveled at those things which were told them by the shepherds. But Mary kept all these things and pondered them in her heart. Then the shepherds returned, glorifying and praising God for all the things that they had heard and seen, as it was told them. (Luke 2:15–20)

Scripture does not tell us how long the heavenly host remained with the shepherds and conducted the unprecedented praise service. The men probably wished it would have gone on for a long time, but very likely it was a brief, intense experience that ended just as suddenly as it began. The angels went back to heaven, took up their places around the throne of God, and resumed praising Him for the grace of salvation.

As traumatic as the experience was—they were literally frightened out of their wits—the shepherds were still able to regather their senses and collect their thoughts after the angels departed. Spontaneously they all had the same response, and the Greek of Luke 2:15 indicates an ongoing kind of discussion in which they reiterated again and again their desire to go to Bethlehem and verify what the angels had announced.

No one had to prod the shepherds into the right response to the divine messengers' words. They were in full agreement that nothing would deter them from going immediately to find the newly arrived Savior: "'Let us go straight to Bethlehem then, and see this thing that has happened which the Lord has made known to us'" (v. 15, NASB). Since Bethlehem sits on a ridge, the shepherds most likely had to walk uphill the two miles from the fields to town. So as soon as possible, they set out to "see this thing that has happened."

The word translated "thing" in this passage denotes much more in Greek than it does in English. The term literally means "word" or "reality." The shepherds understood that they had received a word from God, and the reality of it was that Messiah had been born that same day. And the reality was something they could confirm tangibly because the angel gave them a sign to look for, a baby wrapped in cloths and lying in a manger (2:12). The shepherds had seen and believed the angels, which was sufficient verification for what had occurred, but they wanted to obtain additional authentication by finding the Child exactly where the first angel said He would be. That would affirm their eagerness of faith and prove that they were participants in more than a mere earthly drama.

THE SHEPHERDS RESPOND IN FAITH

It's clear that the shepherds had a revelation from God and equally clear that they wholeheartedly believed it. Their supernaturally wrought experience and their obedient, faithful response are really analogous to how people come to saving faith in Jesus Christ. Salvation comes by hearing a message from God, by hearing and believing the truth about Christ (Rom. 10:9–10).

The Spirit of God obviously had prepared the shepherds' hearts. As we have already suggested, because God chose those men to be the recipients of the angels' special announcement of Christ's birth, they were almost certainly true Jews, that is, believing Jews. Unlike those who were merely ethnic Jews with a secular outlook, the shepherds genuinely believed in the true God (which meant they had repented of sin and sought God's grace), were among those Jews who waited for Messiah, and were undoubtedly among those who looked for the redemption of Israel.

God used the shepherds' existing hope and knowledge to make them receptive to the good news that the Messiah, their Savior the Lord Jesus, had at last come. Such a faithful response to God's special revelation caused the men to obediently pursue the Christ child. All of that is a wonderful illustration of spiritual truth, further underscored by Luke 2:16, "they came with haste." The original expression denotes enthusiasm and eagerness—the shepherds were in a hurry and very enthusiastic as they sought Mary, Joseph, and the divine baby.

Scripture does not describe how the shepherds' search for the baby Jesus actually unfolded. But it's reasonable to assume that they entered Bethlehem and began asking questions: "Does anybody know about a baby being born here in town?" "Anyone heard about the birth of a boy in the past few hours?" There may have been several babies born in Bethlehem that night, so the shepherds may have knocked on a few doors and found some of the other babies. But of course they were looking for one special baby boy whom they would find lying in a feed trough. Their inquiries no doubt spread rapidly by word of mouth and before long they "found Mary and Joseph, and the Babe lying in a manger" (v. 16). At that moment those humble men of faith knew for certain that the angels' announcement was a word from God. Their search had ended just as He promised it would.

THE SHEPHERDS BEAR WITNESS OF CHRIST

The shepherds' response after finding the Christ child continues our analogy of what happens when God saves people. Anyone who hears and embraces the message of the gospel, as the shepherds did, will then witness to others of its truth. They couldn't help but tell those living in and around Bethlehem what the angels had declared to them that night: "Now when they had seen Him, they made widely known the saying which was told them concerning this Child" (Luke 2:17).

Right after the shepherds made the amazing discovery of the infant Jesus, they must have had an extensive conversation with Mary and Joseph. I can picture those working-class men, overwhelmed with all that had happened to them, hearing Joseph humbly asking them how he and Mary could help them. Each shepherd would then likely have vied to tell his version of the story. And as Joseph and Mary sat quietly listening to accounts of the angel's announcement and the heavenly choir's praise of God for such good news, they must have experienced a great sense of confirmation.

Upon hearing the shepherds recount their experiences, each of Jesus' parents likely reported their own recent experiences of heavenly messengers bearing news of the coming Savior. The similarities in all the stories were striking—the details of God's redemptive plan through the Incarnation providentially came together and reaffirmed to everyone around the manger the truth of His promises.

At that point, the shepherds joined Zacharias, Elizabeth, Joseph, and Mary as parties to the greatest news mankind would ever know. And what was their immediate response? They told the story. They witnessed to everyone they encountered that Christ the Lord had been born, that Jesus the Savior was here.

The small group of shepherds became, in effect, the first New Testament evangelists. They went on their way and repeated the astounding news God's angels had revealed to them, and they also recounted their experience of meeting Mary and Joseph and their son. Those men couldn't restrain themselves. The news the shepherds possessed was the greatest information they had ever heard, far beyond anything their humdrum lives could ever have expected. The joy of their salvation and their eagerness to share it proved beyond any doubt that their experiences were valid and that they had truly found the Messiah.

The Shepherds' Influence on the People

The shepherds' enthusiastic, spontaneous witnessing had a profound effect on those around them. Luke tells us, "all those who heard it marveled at those things which were told them by the shepherds" (2:18). The news the men were spreading created quite a stir among the people; in fact, other meanings for "marveled" are "were amazed" and "were filled with wonder." That was consistent with the kind of reaction people would have to Jesus throughout His later ministry. Christ was an amazing person, and He always caused people to be amazed because they had never met anyone else like Him.

There is also a certain amount of marveling today about Jesus, especially during the Christmas season. People have a certain sense of wonder about the baby Jesus and the entire Nativity story. As a result, some will even give Him a certain amount of respect. But being merely amazed or respectful toward Christ is not the same as having saving faith in Him. The Gospels and the Epistles clearly teach that. So it is sad that right from the time Jesus was born, down to the present, people have reacted to Him more with curiosity than with sincerity leading to salvation.

However, the shepherds offer us a refreshing contrast to that pattern. They received God's revelation through the angels with awe and reverence, genuinely believed what they heard, and ran with earnest excitement and singleness of purpose to see the infant Son of God and to tell others about Him. Wouldn't it be wonderful if we could read that all those whom the shepherds witnessed to went immediately to the manger and believed? But that's not what we see. For the most part, the people around Bethlehem who heard the good news just marveled at it briefly and then went on with their lives.

The Shepherds' Influence on Mary

Mary certainly responded to what had happened in a far more profound way than the amazed people who heard the shepherds' proclamation: "But Mary kept all these things and pondered them in her heart" (Luke 2:19). This statement gives us a good idea of the serious manner in which Mary processed all the momentous events of the previous days and months. It also suggests that Mary's response continued to be one of faith, in keeping with what she would have noticed from the shepherds during their visit to the manger.

As she reviewed the amazing facts of the whole story—an angel told her that as a virgin she would conceive and bear the Son of God, the baby would be the Savior of the world and the rightful heir to the throne of David, and He would be the Messiah and the God-Man—the details reminded her once again how mind-boggling everything was. And undoubtedly they prompted her to ponder all sorts of questions, such as, *What am I to expect out of this child? Will I nurse this child the way any mother would nurse her child? Will I rear this child and have a normal relationship with Him as any mother would with her son? When is He going to start uttering profound theological insights? Is He going to perform miracles and how soon? When will He take hold of His Kingdom? And when will He enter into His glory?*

Anything that would come into a mother's mind—and more, considering her unprecedented situation—must have entered Mary's thoughts. And underlying all of that pondering no doubt was deep reflection about God's redemptive purpose, how He had promised a Savior and that Savior had finally come.

Because her son was perfect, Mary must have loved Jesus as no mother has ever loved a child. And yet she would see Him suffer so profoundly and so unjustly. Eventually she would be present when He was nailed to the cross. Being the mother of the Son of God was not going to be all happiness and ease (Luke 2:34–35). So there was much for Mary to contemplate.

Mary's response should resonate with us and be analogous to our own Christian experience. If you are saved, you will first identify with the shepherds' fourfold response of receiving God's revelation, believing the gospel, finding Christ, and witnessing joyfully for Him. But after those early days of euphoria, as you grow in your Christian life, you will also begin to think more deeply about who Jesus is. If you have been a Christian for any length of time, you ought to have an insatiable desire to know more about the Lord, to plumb the depths of Scripture, and to ponder the significance of its truths and how they bear witness to the person and work of Christ. As the apostle Paul wrote, "that I may know Him" (Phil. 3:10; John 17:3; 2 Cor. 4:6; 1 John 5:20). Mary illustrates so well that hungry heart that wants to know Jesus Christ better and understand the depth of His great salvation more fully.

THE SHEPHERDS MOVE ON TO AN OBEDIENT LIFE

The Gospel of Luke does not tell us exactly what the shepherds' attitude was like prior to their incredible encounter with God's revelation. But their attitude certainly changed afterward. Whereas they may have been worried, doubtful, full of questions, and wearied by their daily existence and their feeble attempts to trust God, after their encounter with the angels and the newborn Jesus, they returned to the fields praising and glorifying God. That too is analogous to our experience following conversion. Once we're past the initial stages, we reach a life attitude marked by praise and worship to God.

By the time the shepherds put together the entire astounding story of Christ's birth that night, all the sights, sounds, and words of testimony overwhelmed them and filled them with awe and gratitude. Thus they went back home praising and glorifying God for everything that occurred.

The shepherds without doubt became obedient to God's command that believers live lives characterized by continual rendering of praise and glory to Him (Eph. 5:17–20; Col. 3:15–17; 1 Thess. 5:16–18). Those men could not restrain themselves—because of their salvation, their lives were filled with genuine praise, thankfulness, and worship to God.

In the days immediately following Jesus' birth, Mary and Joseph added to the shepherds' picture of obedience with their own submission to God's will: "And when eight days were completed for the circumcision of the Child, His name was called JESUS, the name given by the angel before He was conceived in the womb" (Luke 2:21).

We shouldn't be surprised that Joseph and Mary had their Son circumcised and named Him Jesus. God's Law required that boys born in Israel be circumcised on the eighth day (Gen. 17:11–12; Lev. 12:1–3). And Gabriel the angel of God had told them to name the boy *Jesus* (Matt. 1:21; Luke 1:31).

But why would Jesus, the Son of God, need to be circumcised? It was necessary because His desire, even as an infant, was to obey God's Law and fulfill all righteousness (Matt. 3:15). Jesus would be a man in every sense, and therefore He would fulfill *all* the requirements listed in the Law for God's people. Even before His Son could consciously comply, God the Father made sure that His earthly parents fulfilled every Old Testament requirement for His life. Jesus' circumcision was simply a preview to what Luke envisioned when he later wrote, "And Jesus increased in wisdom and stature, and in favor with God and men" (2:52). (We'll discuss Jesus' circumcision more completely in chapter 9.)

The shepherds' various responses to Christ's birth and Joseph and Mary's love and obedience in the days immediately following really do encompass a pattern that illustrates the Christian life. You first hear the revelation of the gospel and believe it. Then you pursue and embrace Christ. And having become a witness to your glorious conversion, you begin to tell others about it.

Once you reach that stage as a believer, you start to think more deeply about the significance of being a child of God. You study and ponder God's Word and become a lover of its truths. That leads to a profound sense of joy, praise, and gratitude to God, expressed both in your private and corporate worship. Finally, you continually want to respond in faith and obedience to everything the Lord shows you and teaches you, just as the shepherds, Joseph and Mary, and the child Jesus did.

May God grant you those life-changing spiritual experiences and the ongoing attitude of enthusiasm and responsiveness that cause you to tell others you have seen Christ the Lord.

8

The News Travels Fast

Chapter Eight

∞

The News Travels Fast

I**T'S HARD TO IMAGINE** that anything could rival in importance, interest, and excitement the events that occurred during the hours and days immediately following the birth of Christ. But even several months after the amazing stir created by the angels and shepherds to herald His arrival, people were still hearing about and responding to news of Christ's birth. By that time, men of wealth and influence were reacting to the news coming out of Bethlehem. But was their response any more uniformly noble than that of the shepherds and common people we saw in our previous chapter? Not necessarily. Actually, as you will see, the response of some powerful people was outwardly much worse than the fleeting, indifferent curiosity the average people had to the shepherds' witness. But as with the shepherds and Jesus' parents, some also rendered genuine faith and worship to the newborn King.

In fact, a passage in the other detailed Gospel account of our Lord's birth (Matt. 1:18–2:23) contains examples of three basic responses people of every locale and historical era have typically had toward Him: hostility, indifference, and worship. Matthew 2:1–12 outlines the attitudes this way in the familiar story of the wise men, or Magi:

Now after Jesus was born in Bethlehem of Judea in the days of Herod the king, behold, wise men from the East came to Jerusalem, saying, "Where is

He who has been born King of the Jews? For we have seen His star in the East and have come to worship Him."

When Herod the king heard this, he was troubled, and all Jerusalem with him. And when he had gathered all the chief priests and scribes of the people together, he inquired of them where the Christ was to be born.

So they said to him, "In Bethlehem of Judea, for thus it is written by the prophet:

'But you, Bethlehem, in the land of Judah,
Are not the least among the rulers of Judah;
For out of you shall come a Ruler
Who will shepherd My people Israel.' "

Then Herod, when he had secretly called the wise men, determined from them what time the star appeared. And he sent them to Bethlehem and said, "Go and search carefully for the young Child, and when you have found Him, bring back word to me, that I may come and worship Him also."

When they heard the king, they departed; and behold, the star which they had seen in the East went before them, till it came and stood over where the young Child was. When they saw the star, they rejoiced with exceedingly great joy. And when they had come into the house, they saw the young Child with Mary His mother, and fell down and worshiped Him. And when they had opened their treasures, they presented gifts to Him: gold, frankincense, and myrrh.

Then, being divinely warned in a dream that they should not return to Herod, they departed for their own country another way.

THE MAGI SEEK JESUS

The story of the wise men, or Magi, is a well-known Bible narrative, yet over the centuries a certain amount of myth and tradition has clouded and romanticized it. For instance, a medieval understanding of the story claimed the men were kings, three in number and named Casper, Balthazar, and Melchior. Some believed they represented Noah's three sons; therefore, paintings and drawings depicted one as an Ethiopian. One twelfth-century church leader even claimed to have discovered the Magi's skulls.

However, the only credible facts we know about those men are the few details Matthew provided. He did not choose to tell us their precise number, names, means of transportation, or the specific areas they were from. Matthew's original audience would have known the wise men were from the East, because people generally knew such Magi made up the priestly-political class of the Parthians—who resided east of Palestine.

The Magi date from the seventh century B.C., when they were a tribe within the Median nation of eastern Mesopotamia. They became skilled in astronomy and astrology (which were more closely associated disciplines in those days) and had a sacrificial system somewhat similar to the Mosaic one. We derive the English words *magic* and *magician* from the name *magi*.

The Book of Daniel reports that the Magi, with their knowledge of science, agriculture, mathematics, history, and the occult, were among the highest ranking, most influential officials in the Babylonian Empire. Because of Daniel's own high position and place of respect among them (Dan. 2:24, 48), the Magi undoubtedly learned much from him about the true God and His plans for the Jews through the coming Messiah. Because many Jews remained in Babylon after the Exile, it's likely those teachings remained strong in the region even until New Testament times.

The "wise men from the East" (Matt. 2:1) who came to see Jesus were true Magi who had learned about the Jews' messianic expectations, likely from the prophetic writings such as Daniel's. They were probably among the many God-fearing Gentiles who lived in the Middle East and Mediterranean areas at that time, some of whom—such as Cornelius and Lydia (Acts 10:1–2; 16:14)—are mentioned in the New Testament.

Matthew tells us that when the Magi—whether three or more, he doesn't specify—arrived in Jerusalem, they began the final stage of their search for the Christ child by asking, " 'Where is He who has been born

King of the Jews?'" (2:2). The Greek grammar of that question suggests the men went around the city posing that inquiry to whomever they met. They evidently assumed that if they as foreigners knew about the historic birth, anyone in Judea, and especially Jerusalem, would know where the special baby lived. It was no doubt shocking to the Magi when no one seemed to know what they were talking about.

We don't know how God revealed the birth of Christ to the Magi. Matthew simply says that He gave them the sign of "His [Christ's] star in the East." The identity of that star has stirred perhaps more speculation over the years than has the identity of the men who saw it. Some scholars have proposed it was Jupiter, the largest planet in the solar system. Other commentators have insisted it was the conjunction of Jupiter and Saturn, which formed the sign of the fish, the symbol for Christianity later adopted by the early church. Other conjecture regarding the star's identity has concluded it was probably some other astronomical rarity such as a low-altitude meteor or erratic comet. Some writers have even gone so far as to suggest the phenomenon was some inner vision the Magi had of a "star of destiny" that symbolized mankind's hopes for a savior.

Because Scripture does not explain or identify the star, we can't be dogmatic about its character. It may simply have been the glory of the Lord—the same as the shepherds saw earlier when the angels appeared to them (Luke 2:9). The Bible often equates the manifestation of God's glory with some form of light (Exod. 13:21; 24:17; 34:30; Matt. 17:2; Acts 9:3; 26:13; Rev. 1:16; 21:23). When Moses wrote the Pentateuch, he referred to Messiah as "'a Star [that] shall come out of Jacob'" (Num. 24:17). At the end of the New Testament, Christ called Himself "'the Bright and Morning Star'" (Rev. 22:16).

Therefore it's plausible to say that the extremely bright star, visible only to those for whom God intended it—such as the Magi—was most likely the glory of God. Just as the cloudy pillar of His Shekhinah glory gave light to Israel but darkness to Egypt (Exod. 14:20), God allowed only the wise men to see His glory, depicted in the star's brilliant light over Bethlehem.

It's also quite likely that the Magi were not following the star their entire journey because they had to ask where Jesus was born. It was not until the Jews told them of the prophesied place of Christ's birth that the star reappeared and guided them on to Bethlehem and the exact spot where the baby lay (Matt. 2:9).

The Magi made their long journey west to Palestine for one stated purpose: They wanted to find the newborn Savior and worship Him. "Worship" expresses the idea of falling down and kissing the feet or the hem of the garment of the one honored. That definition in itself verifies that the wise men were true seekers after God. Though they had limited spiritual light, they immediately recognized God's voice when He spoke to them, and they responded in faith and obedience. The Magi had the type of genuine seeking hearts that God promises always to reward (Jer. 29:13).

HEROD'S ANXIETY TOWARD CHRIST

Herod's response to news of Christ's birth was the very opposite of the wise men's: "When Herod the king heard this, he was troubled, and all Jerusalem with him" (Matt. 2:3). The king's anxiety, in contrast to the Magi's joy and eagerness, is understandable. He had expelled the Parthians from Palestine but was again battling Jewish zealots who wanted their country free from Roman domination. Herod was known as a man of intense jealousy and paranoia, so any mention of a potentially rival king of the Jews caused him much fear and anger.

This Herod, known as "the Great," is the first of several New Testament Herods. Under their occupation of Judea, the Romans had appointed his father, Herod Antipater, governor of the region. Antipater then managed to get his son named prefect of Galilee. As prefect, Herod successfully quelled the rebellious Jewish guerillas that still opposed Rome, but he had to flee to Egypt when the Parthians invaded Palestine. Herod returned to Palestine a short while later with stronger backing from Rome as the newly proclaimed "king of the Jews." That's when he fought the Parthians for two years, defeated them, and set up his own kingdom.

Because the Magi were either Parthians or closely associated with the

Parthians, Herod likely had an extra cause for concern. He no doubt viewed the impressive entourage (it probably numbered more than the traditional "three kings"), with its wealth, prestige, and powerful-looking royal demeanor, as a renewed political and military threat from the East.

The Magi's claim to have come simply to worship the newborn King and their earnest desire to find Him obviously did not affect Herod positively. Because it was then common for Magi and other influential leaders to worship kings and emperors, Herod would have cynically thought their mission was as much political as religious.

Herod's first response to news of the wise men's arrival was to summon the Jewish leaders, the chief priests and scribes, and find out from them where the Messiah was to be born. Though Herod was an Idumean (Edomite), he knew Jewish beliefs and customs rather well and associated the title "King of the Jews" with the Jewish Messiah, or Christ. But his awareness of the Jews' hope for a Messiah did not translate into saving faith in Jesus Christ. Instead, the king gave the Magi a disingenuous rationale for wanting to hear from them the precise location and true identity of the infant Jesus—" 'that I may come and worship Him also' " (Matt. 2:8).

Herod's true purpose in wanting to find out where Jesus lived became starkly clear in how he actually responded when the Magi did not report back to him. The Magi were simply obedient to the Lord's leading (2:12), but Herod obeyed his depraved nature and ordered his soldiers to slaughter every male child two years old and under in the vicinity of Bethlehem (v. 16). Of course, by perpetrating such a heinous act, Herod displayed his real desire of wanting to "guarantee" that no newborn king would rival his authority.

Like many hardhearted people today, Herod's immediate response of hateful rebellion and opposition toward Christ shows he really wanted to know nothing of God's way except how to eliminate it. Such an attitude reveals a heart of pride, self-interest, and a greed for power and prestige. Jesus Himself later warned about the consequences of that approach: "'For whoever desires to save his life will lose it. . . . For what profit is it to a man if he gains the whole world, and loses his own soul? Or what will a man give in exchange for his soul?'" (Matt. 16:25–26).

THE INDIFFERENCE OF THE RELIGIOUS LEADERS

There is a third response people have to Christ—indifference. In the story of the wise men, the Jewish religious leaders, composed primarily of the chief priests and scribes, typify such an attitude.

All Jewish priests were of the priestly tribe of Levi, but the chief priests, including the high priest, the captain of the temple, and other temple officials, were the most influential ones. They formed a priestly aristocracy in Israel and in certain ways were similar to the Magi, mainly because they wielded considerable political as well as religious power.

The scribes were primarily Pharisees and were also referred to as the lawyers. They had much prestige and respect among the Jews, who recognized them as scholars and authorities concerning scriptural and traditional Jewish Law. Except for the Sadducees, they held a conservative, literal view of Scripture, and they were very legalistic regarding the ceremonial and moral Law.

As we noted above, Herod called those leaders together to learn more specifically what Jewish Scripture taught about the birthplace of Messiah. The chief priests and scribes answered Herod's question by quoting Micah 5:2 and referring partially to Genesis 49:10: "So they said to him, 'In Bethlehem of Judea, for thus it is written by the prophet: "But you, Bethlehem, in the land of Judah, are not the least among the rulers of Judah; for out of you shall come a Ruler who will shepherd My people Israel"'" (Matt. 2:5–6). That answer was consistent with the concept of a shepherd's being a ruler and therefore fit the intent of Micah's original prophecy. He foresaw that Christ would be the legitimate King of the Jews and also the final and perfect Ruler of Israel.

In human terms, it was to their credit that the unbelieving Jewish leaders were aware that the Old Testament clearly identified a historical figure, the Son of Man, who would be born in Bethlehem and who would come to rule Israel—the Messiah. But sadly, they refused to accept Jesus as that Messiah, not when He was born, not when He ministered among them, and not when He suffered, died, and rose from the grave.

That group of religious experts did not have a perfect idea of what Christ would be like or of what He would do, but they certainly knew enough to recognize Him when He came. Thus, they knew they should follow the Magi's example and worship the newborn Messiah in Bethlehem. They had an intellectual knowledge of God's promises, but the chief priests and scribes were spiritually unmoved when the wise men, prompted by the extraordinary sign of the star, signaled fulfillment of His Word.

Unquestionably, the Jewish leaders are examples of those who are essentially indifferent to God and His program. The prophet Jeremiah lamented over the attitude of such people: "Is it nothing to you, all you who pass by?" (Lam. 1:12). They do not believe or obey what they know of God but at best give Him only lip service. Such apathetic people almost invariably become like Herod and display their hostility toward Christ. That's because indifference to God is simply concealed hatred and delayed rejection.

THE MAGI WORSHIP CHRIST

The wise men, in contrast to Herod and the Jewish leaders, had the kind of attitude that pleases God. They responded to Jesus Christ the way He desires all people to respond—in adoration and worship. Because they had little of the written Word of God, the Magi had much less knowledge of the true God than did the chief priests and scribes. However, those Gentile leaders were remarkably responsive to God's Spirit, and whatever knowledge of God and Christ He revealed to them they believed and followed.

The Magi went on to Bethlehem, not merely because Herod ordered them to, but because finally they were sure they would find the Christ child there. Presumably Herod told them what the religious leaders told him regarding the location of Christ's birth. But the Lord soon gave them much more graphic assistance and confirmation that they were headed in the right direction. "Behold, the star which they had seen in the East went before them, till it came and stood over where the young

Child was" (Matt. 2:9). (That the star hovered directly over the house where Jesus and His family then lived—an impossible action for a normal star—is another strong indicator that it was not an astronomical body, but instead represented the glory of God.)

The men from the East were ecstatic to see the extraordinary star again: "When they saw the star, they rejoiced with exceedingly great joy" (v. 10). Matthew's description uses extra superlatives as if to emphasize the degree of exhilaration the Magi felt. Such emotions reveal once again their uniquely strong interest in finding and worshiping the newly arrived King.

By the time the wise men were journeying to Bethlehem, Jesus and His parents had moved from the travelers' shelter into a house, where they lived until God gave them further direction. There the men finally saw the Child they had traveled so far to find, and they immediately "fell down and worshiped Him" (v. 11). Charles Wesley captured the essence of their experience in these lines from his beautiful Christmas hymn: "Veiled in flesh the Godhead see; hail the incarnate deity; pleased as man with men to dwell, Jesus our Emmanuel."

As an expression of the Magi's grateful worship, "they presented gifts to Him: gold, frankincense, and myrrh" (v. 11). Gold had long been and still is the universal symbol of material wealth and value. It was also a symbol of nobility and royalty, and thus the Magi were appropriately giving Christ the King royal gifts of gold.

Frankincense was an expensive, sweet-smelling incense used for only the most special occasions. Traditionally, it was the incense of deity. In Old Testament times, the Jews stored it in a special chamber in front of the temple and sprinkled it on certain offerings to symbolize the people's desire to please the Lord.

Myrrh was a valuable perfume that some interpreters say represented the gift for a mortal. Therefore its role among the Magi's gifts was to underscore Christ's humanity. The Gospels later record that people mixed myrrh with wine to make an anesthetic (Mark 15:23). Myrrh was also used with spices to prepare bodies for burial, even Jesus' body (John 19:39).

With their mission of finding and worshiping the King of the Jews completed, God warned the Magi in a dream not to report back to Herod. So they returned to the East by a route that allowed them to completely escape the king's notice. Because of the nature and size of the Magi's traveling party, that feat was not easily accomplished. But the Lord guided their steps and granted them wisdom to succeed, further indicating that the wise men's dramatic role in marking the birth of Christ was by divine design.

The Magi's exemplary performance again reminds us that their response to Jesus' birth was the God-honoring one, in contrast to the responses of Herod and the religious leaders. The Magi believed in God's Son, the King of kings, when they heard about Him. Such people today might have little divine light initially, but because they realize it is His light, they respond to the Holy Spirit (2 Cor. 3:6), repent, believe, obey, worship, and live.

9

Righteous Parents ·

Chapter Nine

❦

Righteous Parents

MANY LOCAL TELEVISION STATIONS across the United States entitle their newscasts *Eyewitness News*. Obviously, the impression station managers and news directors want to convey is that their newscasts are accurate and that viewers can count on the broadcasts as bona fide sources of daily community information. Such telecasts do not always achieve their goals of accuracy and balanced reporting, but use of the term *eyewitness* by the producers implies a desire to attain those ideals. That's because *eyewitness,* in some sense, still connotes the idea of a credible, reliable report—a trustworthy individual actually witnessed certain events and can provide a truthful account of them.

The principle of the honest eyewitness also derives from the traditions and standards of Western jurisprudence. Courts accept a story as true when two or three witnesses can corroborate and verify its major elements. But the principle goes back much further to the biblical affirmation that testimony had to be confirmed in the mouth of two or three witnesses (Num. 35:30; Deut. 17:6; Matt. 18:16; 1 Tim. 5:19).

Luke, ever the careful historian and theologian, used the testimony of reliable witnesses to great effect in confirming the truth of his narrative of the birth of Christ. His efforts were all the more effective because he could cite the most credible witnesses any writer ever had. And he did all that so we would know beyond a doubt that Jesus Christ was the greatest and most special child ever born.

THE RIGHTEOUSNESS OF JOSEPH AND MARY

First of all, Luke removed any uncertainty about the character and honesty of his witnesses by relying on the testimony of Jesus' parents. Because of the righteous character of Joseph and Mary's lives, Luke knew his readers could trust their testimony.

Matthew 1:19 identifies Joseph this way: "Joseph . . . being a just man." That means he was right with God—a righteous man. And that was notable because in those days Israel had quite an array of theological and political viewpoints that were out of step with God's righteous plan. There were those influenced by the Sadducees, who were essentially the religious liberals (they denied the supernatural and a bodily resurrection from the dead). Many Jews followed the system of the religious legalists, the Pharisees, who believed in tradition, ceremonies, and good works as a means to salvation. Then there were the adherents of nationalism, who politicized Judaism and were fanatically intent on overthrowing Roman control and regaining independence for the nation of Israel. The Zealots most clearly represented that outlook. And there was even a segment of Jewish society that lived out in the desert as separatists. The Essenes, with their asceticism and contemplative piety, epitomized that sectarian element.

Those crosscurrents of unscriptural emphases had led the nation of Israel far from God. But He was still working among a small remnant of His people, reassuring them that Messiah was coming and that His plan of redemption was still intact. The Lord was faithfully carrying out His program through righteous people, those who believed His promises, repented of their sins, and cast themselves on His mercy for the forgiveness of sins. Joseph was a prime example of this righteous remnant, as was his young wife, Mary, whom Luke earlier quoted as saying, "'My soul magnifies the Lord, and my spirit has rejoiced in God my Savior'" (1:46–47). It's clear that Jesus' parents knew and loved the Lord.

THE TESTIMONY OF JOSEPH AND MARY

Joseph and Mary's devotion to follow the will of God in everything pertaining to their new son was also clear. Luke 2:21–24 features that faithful, joyful spirit of obedience:

> And when eight days were completed for the circumcision of the Child, His name was called JESUS, the name given by the angel before He was conceived in the womb.
>
> Now when the days of her purification according to the law of Moses were completed, they brought Him to Jerusalem to present Him to the Lord (as it is written in the law of the Lord, "Every male who opens the womb shall be called holy to the LORD"), and to offer a sacrifice according to what is said in the law of the Lord, "A pair of turtledoves or two young pigeons."

The Circumcising and Naming of Jesus

The first way in which Jesus' parents testified to His identity as Messiah and Savior was by bringing Him to be circumcised and formally named.

The Law of Moses prescribed that the parents of male babies, when the boys were eight days old, were to have their sons circumcised (Lev. 12:3). However, God first introduced the rite of circumcision (Gen. 17:9–14) to Abraham when he underwent the formal procedure as an adult and the Lord identified him as the father of the Israelite nation. From then on, as a sign of the covenant, every male child in Israel was to be circumcised on the eighth day.

Although circumcision was physical and done for health reasons (by having the man's foreskin cut away, God was protecting the Jewish wife from receiving harmful infections and bacteria from her husband), it primarily symbolized the need for spiritual cleansing. Every time Jewish parents brought a son to be circumcised, it was a reminder of original sin—they were sinners; they had borne a sinner—and their need for a cleansing at the deepest level of their souls. That's why Scripture commands us to circumcise our hearts (Rom. 2:28–29; Phil. 3:3; Col. 2:11).

But why did Jesus, the holy and sinless Son of God (Isa. 53:9; 2 Cor. 5:21), need to be circumcised? Because that's what God's Law required. Whatever His Law mandated at that time in redemptive history, Jesus, through His earthly parents, wanted to comply with those commands. As the apostle Paul wrote, "God sent forth His Son, born of a woman, born under the law" (Gal. 4:4).

Christ came to fulfill every aspect of the Law (Matt. 5:17), whether He did so passively as an infant at His circumcision or actively as an adult at His baptism. "Then Jesus came from Galilee to John at the Jordan to be baptized by him. And John tried to prevent Him, saying, 'I need to be baptized by You, and are You coming to me?' But Jesus answered and said to him, 'Permit it to be so now, for thus it is fitting for us to fulfill all righteousness.' Then he allowed Him" (Matt. 3:13–15).

Jesus entered this world and lived obediently as a child, young person, and adult under the Law—an entire life of perfection—so that at the Cross the Father could credit the Son's perfect life to sinners' accounts. Without the death of One who lived a perfect life, there could be no substitutionary atonement. At Calvary, God treated Jesus as if He had lived your life so He could treat you as if you had lived Jesus' life. That is a simple summary of the doctrine of justification.

According to Jewish custom, the parents named the son at the same time they had him circumcised. So on that occasion Christ's parents formally named Him Jesus—and the choice of that name was an easy one. The angel had told both Joseph and Mary that they were to name their Son *Jesus* (Matt. 1:21; Luke 1:31).

Jesus is the New Testament equivalent of the Hebrew name *Joshua* and means "Yahweh saves." Joshua, Moses' successor, was a great deliverer (Deut. 31:1–8; Josh. 1:1–7) who led the people of Israel into the Promised Land. But the Child whom Mary and Joseph named *Jesus* was a far greater Deliverer than Joshua. He was God the Savior, come in human flesh to willingly and compassionately save all those who believe.

God is by nature a saving God (Ezek. 18:23, 32), and Jesus demonstrated those sympathies when He wept over the lost condition of

Jerusalem: "'O Jerusalem, Jerusalem, the one who kills the prophets and stones those who are sent to her! How often I wanted to gather your children together, as a hen gathers her chicks under her wings, but you were not willing!'" (Matt. 23:37; Matt. 11:28; Luke 15:11–32).

Christianity, as the world's only true religion, is the only one that provides a genuine savior, and that Savior is Jesus. He affirmed that when He declared, "'For the Son of Man has come to seek and to save that which was lost'" (Luke 19:10). And Joseph and Mary testified to that truth when they named Him at His circumcision.

Jesus Presented to God after Mary's Purification

The second aspect of Joseph and Mary's testimony to Jesus was twofold: Mary observed a prescribed time of purification for herself, and she and Joseph formally presented Jesus to God. "Now when the days of her purification according to the law of Moses were completed, they brought Him to Jerusalem to present Him to the Lord (as it is written in the law of the Lord, 'Every male who opens the womb shall be called holy to the Lord'), and to offer a sacrifice according to what is said in the law of the Lord, 'A pair of turtledoves or two young pigeons'" (Luke 2:22–24).

As Luke tells us, Mary observed a set time for personal purification, in keeping with the Mosaic Law. In Leviticus 12:2–4, the Lord commanded Moses, "'Speak to the children of Israel, saying: "If a woman has conceived, and borne a male child, then she shall be unclean seven days; as in the days of her customary impurity she shall be unclean. And on the eighth day the flesh of his foreskin shall be circumcised. She shall then continue in the blood of her purification thirty-three days. She shall not touch any hallowed thing, nor come into the sanctuary until the days of her purification are fulfilled."'"

The seven-day uncleanness was a ceremonial uncleanness that meant the woman could not enter the tabernacle (later the temple) or touch anything holy during that time. The week was symbolically parallel to the woman's monthly menstrual period, during which God also considered her unclean. Both types of uncleanness were regular reminders to the woman and to her family that they were still sinners in need of God's forgiveness.

Beginning on the eighth day, the new mother of a male child had to face another period of uncleanness, the thirty-three days of her purification. As in the previous seven days, she was not to touch any consecrated item or enter the worship sanctuary. So for Mary and all other obedient Jewish women who bore sons, there was a somewhat bittersweet forty-day period. On the one hand, they experienced the great joy of having a new son, which meant the family name would continue. But on the other hand, they had to endure a mandatory disassociation from holy things as a reminder that they were sinners, that they had borne sinful sons, and therefore that as human mothers, they needed purification.

Once Mary had carefully observed and completed the forty-day period of uncleanness, she could joyfully and with a clear conscience present Jesus to the Lord. She was accompanied by Joseph, which meant the entire little family was present at the temple for the special observance of the completion of Mary's purification.

As with the circumcision and purification, Joseph and Mary obeyed the Old Testament when they presented their Son to God: "The first-born of your sons you shall give to Me" (Exod. 22:29; 13:2, 12, 15; Num. 8:17). It was not mandatory for them to go to the Temple to present Jesus. But in the spirit of how Hannah brought Samuel to the Lord (1 Sam. 1:24–28), they went above and beyond the normal duty and brought God's Son to God's house. They knew the Child was very special and that He, of all children, belonged to the Lord already. By their action Jesus' parents in effect said, "We are devoting this Child to You, God. He is already Yours, so do whatever You will in His life so He serves, honors, and glorifies You."

That special presentation did not mean, however, that Joseph and Mary dedicated Jesus to the Levitical priesthood. They were of the tribe of Judah and therefore, like all non-Levite families, they needed to redeem their Son from that priestly responsibility by paying five shekels of silver (Num. 18:15–16). That would have been equivalent to many days' wages, a difficult amount for a working-class couple like Joseph and Mary to pay. But God made sure they had the necessary coins.

That Jesus the Redeemer was ceremonially redeemed is an interesting irony, but it is nevertheless an important scriptural reality. Just as with His earlier circumcision and later baptism, Jesus did not need to go through any picture of redemption. He was the sinless Son of God; He did not need to be cleansed from sin or redeemed from condemnation. But He was circumcised, He was baptized, and He was "redeemed" as part of His presentation to God—all because He had to obey the letter of the Law to fulfill all righteousness on our behalf.

The Sacrifice for Mary's Purification

Jesus' ceremonial dedication to the Lord by His parents, as significant as it was, did not officially end Mary's time of uncleanness. That end would come only by her offering a sacrifice for purification. And once again Mary, as a righteous woman, followed God's original pattern for offering such a sacrifice:

> When the days of her purification are fulfilled, whether for a son or a daughter, she shall bring to the priest a lamb of the first year as a burnt offering, and a young pigeon or a turtledove as a sin offering, to the door of the tabernacle of meeting. Then he shall offer it before the LORD, and make atonement for her. And she shall be clean from the flow of her blood. This is the law for her who has borne a male or a female.
>
> And if she is not able to bring a lamb, then she may bring two turtledoves or two young pigeons—one as a burnt offering and the other as a sin offering. So the priest shall make atonement for her, and she will be clean. (Lev. 12:6–8)

Notice that Mary had several options in offering her sacrifice. If she and Joseph had had the resources, they could have brought a lamb and a bird. But since they couldn't afford to do that, they utilized the second option and brought a pair of birds (Luke 2:24). That indicates again that Mary and Joseph were not wealthy. However, the Lord enabled them, with their middle-class resources, to purchase the two birds in the temple, even at inflated prices.

After the priest made atonement for Mary by sacrificing the birds—one for a burnt offering, the other for a sin offering—she was clean. That didn't mean the blood of the sacrifices washed her sins away; it simply meant Mary's heart was then right with the Lord because she had confessed her sin and impurity and asked Him for forgiveness.

The sacrifice for Mary's purification was a wonderful picture that looked ahead to her Son's final sacrifice, which alone can actually remove people's sin. When Christ was sacrificed on the cross, God revealed the only answer for sinful alienation from Him. Remember what happened right after Jesus' death? The thick temple veil that separated mankind from God was ripped in two from top to bottom. That momentous event signified there was now access to God because the final atoning sacrifice was complete. Never again would repentant sinners, such as Mary, need to deal with ceremonial uncleanness.

So Joseph and Mary gave the first confirming testimony to Jesus' birth, identity, and true purpose. They named Him Jesus because they knew He would save His people from their sins. They came to the temple (which they didn't have to do) and offered Him to God because they understood that, in a special way, He belonged to the Lord. They had that understanding, of course, because they knew their newborn was the Christ, the Son of the Father.

Because of Joseph and Mary's faithful testimony, we also can know that the Babe born in Bethlehem was and is the Son of God, the Redeemer of all who trust in Him.

10

Simeon's Eyes of Faith

Chapter Ten

Simeon's Eyes of Faith

A FORGOTTEN AUTHORITY on Wesleyan hymns once commented, "There can hardly be a single paragraph of Scripture that is not somewhere reflected in the hymns of the Wesleys." That observation was certainly accurate regarding the following two stanzas from Charles Wesley's elegant 1744 Advent hymn:

> Come, Thou long-expected Jesus, Born to set Thy people free;
> From our fears and sins release us; Let us find our rest in Thee.
> Israel's strength and consolation, Hope of all the earth Thou art;
> Dear Desire of ev'ry nation, Joy of ev'ry longing heart.
>
> Born Thy people to deliver, Born a Child, and yet a King,
> Born to reign in us forever, Now Thy gracious kingdom bring.
> By Thine own eternal Spirit Rule in all our hearts alone;
> By Thine all-sufficient merit, Raise us to Thy glorious throne.

Those beautiful lines summarize well the main sentiments of another impeccable testimony to the significance and validity of Christ's birth—the aged, humble, and wise Simeon. Luke again reports on what happened and records Simeon's prophetic words:

And behold, there was a man in Jerusalem whose name was Simeon, and this man was just and devout, waiting for the Consolation of Israel, and the Holy Spirit was upon him. And it had been revealed to him by the Holy Spirit that he would not see death before he had seen the Lord's Christ. So he came by the Spirit into the temple. And when the parents brought in the Child Jesus, to do for Him according to the custom of the law, he took Him up in his arms and blessed God and said:

"Lord, now You are letting Your servant depart in peace,
According to Your word;
For my eyes have seen Your salvation
Which You have prepared before the face of all peoples,
A light to bring revelation to the Gentiles,
And the glory of Your people Israel."

And Joseph and His mother marveled at those things which were spoken of Him. Then Simeon blessed them, and said to Mary His mother, "Behold, this Child is destined for the fall and rising of many in Israel, and for a sign which will be spoken against (yes, a sword will pierce through your own soul also), that the thoughts of many hearts may be revealed." (2:25–35)

THE MAN SIMEON

Although very little is known about him except what Luke 2 records, Simeon was, as we shall see, a fascinating character. His name is certainly a common Hebrew name (it was the name of one of the twelve tribes of Israel; Gen. 49:5–7) that means, "God has heard." When Simeon's parents named him as a baby, the Lord prompted them to give him a name that wonderfully alludes to the result of his heartfelt cry for God to send a comforter and deliverer. That cry was certainly Simeon's lifelong hope, and at the end of his life God graciously heard and sent the Messiah.

His Spiritual Character

The first biblical description of the man Simeon involves his spiritual character: "this man was just and devout" (Luke 2:25). As we saw regarding Joseph and Mary, that simple statement is loaded with meaning—as a just man, Simeon stood righteous before God. God had declared him righteous, as only God can, when he trusted in Him rather than his good works for the forgiveness of sin. Simeon recognized his sinfulness, cast himself on the mercy of God, and the Lord declared him righteous because Christ's death on the cross would bear away his sins.

If Simeon was a just man, it follows that he was also "devout." That word means he was righteous. If anyone is truly justified, then scripturally he or she is necessarily also righteous, or in the process of being sanctified. Even in Simeon's day, still under the Old Testament economy, when God declared someone like him righteous, that person's life changed and he became a lover of God's Law (see Psalm 119 and David's heart attitude toward the Law of God).

Simply stated, a devout man such as Simeon is primarily concerned about the things of God. In fact, the term rendered "devout" in Luke 2 is often more literally translated "cautious," indicating that Simeon would have been very careful how he treated God and responded to His Word. He lived a careful, cautious, responsible life, one that was exemplary and conscientious to honor God and bring glory to His name. And that's what defined Simeon's character as a true Jew—a believing Jew—and a genuine member of the righteous remnant of Israel.

His Theology

Luke 2:25 also indicates something important about Simeon's theology: he was "waiting for the Consolation of Israel." The word rendered "Consolation" is a direct reference to the Messiah. Thus Simeon had a hope for the coming of Messiah, the King who would bring in the promised Kingdom of Israel. And the only one who could fulfill that hope was the Consoler, the Comforter, the Helper—the Messiah.

But what was the source of Simeon's great sense of hope? Undoubtedly, a major one had to be the Book of Isaiah. The second half of the prophet's inspired writing contains a wealth of references to the theme of the coming Messianic consolation and comfort. Isaiah 40:1–2 declares, "'Comfort, yes, comfort My people!' says your God. 'Speak comfort to Jerusalem, and cry out to her, that her warfare is ended, that her iniquity is pardoned.'" The righteous Jews looked for the time when Israel's warfare would end and the Comforter (Messiah) would remove all sins.

The prophet goes on to say, "Behold, the Lord God shall come with a strong hand, and His arm shall rule for Him; behold, His reward is with Him, and His work before Him. He will feed His flock like a shepherd; He will gather the lambs with His arm, and carry them in His bosom, and gently lead those who are with young" (vv. 10–11). None other than God Himself, in the person of Christ, would come to rule and comfort His people, even as a shepherd helps his sheep and lambs.

Isaiah 49:8–10 provides further promise:

Thus says the LORD:
    "In an acceptable time I have heard You,
    And in the day of salvation I have helped You;
    I will preserve You and give You
    As a covenant to the people,
    To restore the earth,
    To cause them to inherit the desolate heritages;
    That You may say to the prisoners, 'Go forth,'
    To those who are in darkness, 'Show yourselves.'
    "They shall feed along the roads,
    And their pastures shall be on all desolate heights.
    They shall neither hunger nor thirst,
    Neither heat nor sun shall strike them;
    For He who has mercy on them will lead them,
    Even by the springs of water He will guide them."

God in effect reiterated the Abrahamic Covenant and promised to give Israel back her land. And along with that, the Lord pledged to minister a variety of compassionate favors. All of these prophecies foreshadowed the ministry of Christ as the Comforter of His people (Isa. 51:3; 57:18; 66:10–13).

So Simeon was a man who believed the Old Testament and took the prophet's promises of consolation for Israel at face value. Simeon cared not only about his personal salvation, but also about the spiritual welfare of his people. His desire was very much a precursor to Paul's decades later, when the apostle told the Roman believers:

> I tell the truth in Christ, I am not lying, my conscience also bearing me witness in the Holy Spirit, that I have great sorrow and continual grief in my heart. For I could wish that I myself were accursed from Christ for my brethren, my countrymen according to the flesh, who are Israelites, to whom pertain the adoption, the glory, the covenants, the giving of the law, the service of God, and the promises; of whom are the fathers and from whom, according to the flesh, Christ came, who is over all, the eternally blessed God. Amen. (Romans 9:1–5)

In that sense, Simeon was a passionate true believer. And he even went Paul one better. The great apostle was not a member of the true remnant for his entire adult life and ministry; after all, he once persecuted Christians prior to his conversion from legalistic, lost Judaism. But Simeon always looked in faith to the hope of Israel's comfort and consolation, the coming of Messiah. He longed earnestly for the fulfillment of the covenant promises; and the more his nation sank into sin, apostasy, unbelief, and legalism, the more his heart ached to see the Messiah deliver his fellow Israelites from all of that iniquity.

His Special Anointing

In addition to his exemplary character qualities and his adherence to biblical theology, Simeon was a remarkable example of divine anointing for extraordinary service: "the Holy Spirit was upon him" (Luke 2:25).

First of all, Luke's statement about Simeon applies just as if he were speaking of any Old Testament-era believer. The Spirit of God had to work in his heart to save him—to enable him to believe that God would provide a sacrifice and would forgive his sins, and that it was all by grace through faith, not works. The Holy Spirit used the picture of the Old Testament sacrificial system to point Simeon and other true Jews toward Christ's final sacrifice. He thus brought them to justification and began the ongoing process of sanctification in their lives. In Simeon's life we clearly see that process at work in his devout character and careful obedience to God's Law.

That the Holy Spirit was upon Simeon, therefore, was not an indicator of a brand-new phenomenon. The Spirit was always present in believers' lives. Luke was simply saying that God had anointed Simeon for a special responsibility, much as He had done for certain Old Testament saints (e.g., Samson, Samuel, the prophets). Most often that responsibility involved speaking for God, as we'll see when Simeon interacts with the young Jesus and His parents.

But before Simeon uttered any prophetic statements, the Spirit had to reveal certain truths to him. "It had been revealed to him by the Holy Spirit that he would not see death before he had seen the Lord's Christ" (2:26). Sometime earlier in his life God had revealed that amazing message to Simeon, which would have had some rare and unusual implications for his life.

God's words probably created both exhilaration and tension for Simeon. Positively, they would have served as a wonderful milepost or terminus point around which he could have ordered his life. Imagine the incredible feeling of having precise insight into exactly what needed to occur before you could die. But such knowledge also undoubtedly resulted in some spiritual pressure for Simeon. The constant excitement of living in Messianic times and eagerly anticipating the appearance of Christ on any given day, week, or month must have been a powerful motivation for Simeon to examine his heart regularly. He wanted to be sure he was fully ready for the special event. We don't know how long prior to Luke 2 that Simeon had known all those things, but the entire waiting process, however long or short, surely filled his heart with anticipation as he realized Messiah was coming in his lifetime.

SIMEON AT LAST MEETS CHRIST

Simeon's sense of anticipation that he would actually see the Messiah, and his lifelong looking forward in hope to the consolation of Israel, finally culminated on a special day that coincided with Jesus' presentation to the Lord. God providentially prompted his heart, and Simeon decided it was exactly the right time to go down to the temple: "So he came by the Spirit into the temple" (Luke 2:27). More precisely, the word translated "temple" means "big area" and refers to the Court of the Women, the outside courtyard that was the only temple-related place Mary could go.

God in His sovereign wisdom appointed a time and place for Simeon and Christ to meet. And the meeting occurred even though Joseph and Mary knew nothing of Simeon, and he knew nothing of them or how to identify the Child. However, the Lord overcame those barriers and brought the four people together. Perhaps Simeon approached the parents and initiated a conversation in this fashion: "The Spirit of God has led me here and has prompted me that it's where the Messiah is. Can you give me some information?" To which Joseph and Mary may have replied, "Yes, here He is."

Likewise, we can only imagine what Simeon felt as he took the baby Jesus out of Mary's arms, pressed Him to his chest, and perhaps leaned his head down to kiss Him. We can only speculate concerning the magnitude of joy that must have flooded the old man's heart as he realized God truly did fulfill His promises. At last, he was holding in his hands the Messiah, the Comforter and Consoler of Israel, the Savior of the world.

Simeon was filled with such great joy because he genuinely believed that Jesus was the Messiah. And he believed that because Joseph and Mary told him. They undoubtedly reported to him the amazing, miraculous ways in which Jesus' birth had come to pass and reaffirmed to him how God had confirmed the truth of it all to their hearts. Simeon had long believed in the coming Messiah, and God was at that moment rewarding his faith by showing him specifically and unquestionably that the infant Jesus was the Christ.

SIMEON'S SONG OF PRAISE

The moment Simeon realized that the baby he saw and held was indeed the Lord Jesus Christ, the promised Messiah, he launched into one of the most well-known, beloved, and theologically rich songs of praise found in all of Scripture. It certainly marked the most magnificent and joyful moment in his life as he witnessed the fulfillment of God's promise that he would live to see the Messiah. Simeon's clear testimony, known liturgically as the *Nunc Dimittis* (from the opening two words, "now Lord," of the song's Latin translation), appears in four short verses: " 'Lord, now You are letting Your servant depart in peace, according to Your word; for my eyes have seen Your salvation which You have prepared before the face of all peoples, a light to bring revelation to the Gentiles, and the glory of Your people Israel' " (Luke 2:29–32).

Simeon's affirmation that God was letting him depart in peace is simply a Semitic expression that he was then ready to die. He was acknowledging that everything was right for a sovereign God to let him die in peace. And why was that? Because Simeon understood that God is a saving God (1 Tim. 4:10), and that he was seeing the arrival of God's salvation in the person of Jesus, the Messiah (Luke 1:69; Acts 4:12). His praise flowed because God's Savior had come and, therefore, God's salvation had come—and with that great truth a reality, it was then all right for his life to end. Simeon had lived to see what God had promised him.

But Simeon's testimony did not end with one statement. If he had merely added his voice to that of Zacharias, Mary, and Joseph and confirmed the truth of God's salvation for His people, it would not have advanced the testimony about Messiah any further. However, Simeon did go further and prophetically declared a truth that was shattering to conventional Israelite belief: "'For my eyes have seen Your salvation which You have prepared before the face of all peoples, a light to bring revelation to the Gentiles, and the glory of Your people Israel'" (Luke 2:30–32).

Simeon's additional words would have been truly astonishing for most Jews of his day. They believed someone would come as their Messiah, that he would reestablish the Kingdom of Israel, and with that kingdom that he would rule over the infidel Gentile world. But Simeon's bold declaration said that God brought His Messiah/Savior to earth and prepared His salvation for *all peoples* without distinction—it is a light of revelation to the Gentiles, as well as being the glory of Israel.

Simeon's statement was all the more shocking because even the remnant of Israel, those who believed and studied the Old Testament, hated what the term *Gentile* represented—no belief in the Scripture, desecration of the true and living God, disobedience to the commandment to love God above everything else, and violation of the prohibition against worshiping images of other gods. And as Gentiles became a more distinct group within Jewish society, members of the remnant seemed to resent the Gentiles' blasphemy and idolatry more and more.

Even the most faithful and righteous of the believing Jews could not imagine that God's salvation would include people beyond Israel. For example, when the shepherds heard the angels proclaim, "'For there is born *to you* this day in the city of David a Savior, who is Christ the Lord'" (Luke 2:11; emphasis added), they assumed the "to you" meant them and other Jews. And when Mary and Joseph heard they were to name their son Jesus ("Yahweh saves") because He would save His people from their sins, they understood "His people" to mean only Israel.

However, the numerous statements of the prophet Isaiah, uttered centuries earlier, contradicted such thinking. Isaiah 9:1–2 applies to Galilee's honor at the time of Jesus' ministry: "Nevertheless the gloom will not be upon her who is distressed, as when at first He lightly esteemed the land of Zebulun and the land of Naphtali, and afterward more heavily oppressed her, by the way of the sea, beyond the Jordan, in Galilee of the Gentiles. The people who walked in darkness have seen a great light; those who dwelt in the land of the shadow of death, upon them a light has shined." Jesus actually did go to the other side of the Jordan to preach and serve. Those who lived in dark lands (Gentiles) experienced the light of the gospel.

Isaiah 42:6–7 says, "I, the LORD, have called You in righteousness, and will hold Your hand; I will keep You and give You as a covenant to the people, as a light to the Gentiles, to open blind eyes, to bring out prisoners from the prison, those who sit in darkness from the prison house." The prophet recorded a conversation between the Father and the Son that indicated God would use Christ, working through the nation of Israel, to be a light to the nations. That same expression (or one very similar), with the same meaning, appears four other places in the Book of Isaiah (49:6; 51:4; 52:10; 60:1–3; 45:25; 46:13).

In view of all those prophetic statements, no one should have been shocked at Simeon's words. He could have had any one of the Isaiah references in mind with his declaration, which demonstrates again that Simeon was a man of God and a capable spokesman to announce the significance of Christ's birth. In this case the significance is that salvation, brought by Messiah, has been prepared by God to be sufficient for the whole world because He loves the world (Matt. 28:18–20; John 3:16; 1 Tim. 2:1–6; 1 Pet. 3:9).

THE PARENTS' RESPONSE TO SIMEON

As we've seen in our study, Joseph and Mary were already full of wonder and amazement concerning the incredible facts and miraculous circumstances attending the birth of Jesus. They realized they were the earthly parents of the Son of God, the Messiah, and the Savior of His people, all of which was beyond their comprehension. Then when they heard Simeon's statement about the Gentiles, they were astonished anew and reminded afresh that the entire episode was entirely beyond their grasp (Luke 2:33). God had, as it were, placed in Joseph and Mary's hands a Savior for everyone who believes, Jew *and* Gentile.

But the euphoria of that realization ended quickly for Mary and Joseph when Simeon concluded his pronouncement with this final, shocking statement: "'Behold, this Child is destined for the fall and rising of many in Israel, and for a sign which will be spoken against (yes, a sword will pierce through your own soul also), that the thoughts of many hearts may be revealed'" (vv. 34–35).

Jesus' parents surely were taken aback when listening to those words, the tone of which they had not heard before. Simeon's prediction constitutes the first negative note in Luke's account of Christ's birth. Until then it had been all a record of divine promises fulfilled and news of God's salvation that brought a sense of peace, hope, joy, and praise for His glory. But then Jesus' parents, particularly Mary, had to grapple with thoughts of Israelites falling and rising and a sword piercing Mary's soul. They certainly were asking themselves what Simeon's closing words really meant.

Simeon directed his sober forewarning especially to Mary rather than Joseph because he knew Joseph wouldn't be present for the culmination of Jesus' ministry. After Jesus' encounter with the Jewish teachers in the temple when He was twelve, Joseph disappears from the record. (He might have died even before Jesus began His earthly ministry.) But Mary witnessed or heard about all the high moments and low points of her Son's ministry. And Simeon foresees Mary's experience according to three categories: separation, opposition, and affliction.

Christ Separates People

First, Simeon knew Mary would endure emotional conflict, pain, and suffering because Jesus would represent a line of demarcation in the lives of all who saw and heard Him. Some would respond positively and rise to the glories of salvation, but others would respond negatively and fall into the despair of eternal judgment.

Simeon was introducing a new concept. Mary and everyone else who heard his words confronted for the first time the new perspective that some—even many—Jews would be lost. Not all of them would rejoice at Messiah's ministry. Again, Simeon could have drawn his thoughts directly from Isaiah: "'He [Messiah] will be as a sanctuary, but a stone of stumbling and a rock of offense to both the houses of Israel, as a trap and a snare to the inhabitants of Jerusalem. And many among them shall stumble; they shall fall and be broken, be snared and taken'" (8:14–15; 28:16; John 1:11; 1 Pet. 2:6–8).

The life and ministry of Jesus Christ would perfectly verify the words of Simeon and the prophets. The whole nation of Israel turned against our Lord, and ultimately the Jewish leaders persuaded the Romans to have Him executed—only a relatively small remnant of Jews received Him and believed unto eternal life. The rest would fall irretrievably over the "stone of stumbling" and "rock of offense."

Christ Stirs Opposition from People

The division Messiah's life caused among His people included overt opposition from many. He represented the light and righteousness that the average person hated (John 3:18–20). Eventually, as the Gospels clearly attest, the unbelieving Jews would contest everything Jesus said and did. The opposition began with indifference and progressed to hatred, plotting, insults, mockery, verbal vilification, physical torture, and abuse, and it ended with crucifixion.

It is hard enough for us today to believe that many of the Jews in Jesus' time opposed Him so sinfully and completely. But Mary, who heretofore had done nothing but rejoice over the arrival of Messiah, had to be feeling shock and sadness over Simeon's warning. Perhaps it would have been understandable if such future opposition had referred to the Gentiles; but it was unthinkable for her to identify it with the chosen nation of Israel.

But God's sovereign redemptive purpose was again behind Simeon's sobering declaration. His words could have wonderfully clarified for believing Jews like Mary the prophecy of Isaiah 53:3, "He [Christ] is despised and rejected by men, a Man of sorrows and acquainted with grief. And we hid, as it were, our faces from Him; He was despised, and we did not esteem Him."

Mary Experiences Affliction

Simeon's prophecy then turned from addressing the nations to addressing Mary personally. He said, in effect, that before everything ended, Mary's role as Jesus' mother would become very difficult personally. "'A sword will pierce through your own soul also'" (Luke 2:35).

Because Mary undoubtedly loved Jesus more than any mother ever loved a child, it was extremely hard for her when Jesus had to push her away on the human level. When at age twelve He had to be about His Father's business in the temple (Luke 2:46–50), it was necessary, in a sense, to push Mary aside. Later, when He was doing His first miracle in Cana (John 2:1–11), Jesus didn't call her "mother"; He called her "woman" (v. 4). And on another occasion, when Mary came to visit Him with His half brothers (Matt. 12:46–50), He said, "'Who is My mother and who are My brothers?' And He stretched out His hand toward His disciples and said, 'Here are My mother and My brothers! For whoever does the will of My Father in heaven is My brother and sister and mother'" (vv. 48–50).

Jesus gently but firmly nudged Mary from merely being His mother to realizing that she needed to depend on Him as her Savior and Lord. And after Jesus was hated, ridiculed, unfairly tried, physically assaulted, and crucified, Mary was standing at the foot of the cross, watching right up to the end of His life (John 19:25). Seeing Jesus suffering on the cross certainly would have rammed a sword through her maternal heart. In addition, Mary's heart was no doubt pierced through because she, as a believing Jew, had to witness all the unbelieving opposition to Christ pour forth from many of her fellow Israelites.

Mary was an ordinary woman who dealt with enormous strain just being the mother of the Son of God. Her life accurately fulfilled Simeon's admonition to her as she periodically felt bewildered by Jesus' words and actions and certainly cut to the heart with emotional pain as she saw His rejection, suffering, and death.

THE REVELATION SIMEON'S WORDS PREDICT

Years ago I read about a man who took a friend on a tour of Paris. They went to the Louvre and looked at all the great paintings there. That night they went to a concert hall and heard a wonderful symphony. At the end of the evening, the man asked his friend, "Well, what do you think?" And the friend replied, "I wasn't all that impressed."

In response, the man told his friend, "If it's any consolation to you, the museum and its art were not on trial and neither was the symphony. You were on trial. History has already determined the greatness of these works of art and of this music. All that your attitude reveals is the smallness of your own appreciation."

Likewise, Jesus isn't on trial, but every soul is. Simeon declared, "'This Child . . . is a sign which will be spoken against . . . that the thoughts of many hearts may be revealed'" (Luke 2:34–35). When God prompted Jesus to begin His ministry, many people rallied to oppose Him. That opposition simply revealed the wickedness of people's hearts. Specifically, it also revealed the apostasy of the Jews' religion, with all its hypocrisy, self-righteousness, legalism, and shallowness. And that attitude is still prevalent today.

When considering the facts of Christ's birth, many people think, *You know, the baby Jesus was a sweet child. And when He grew up, peace, joy, and happiness followed Him everywhere. Jesus was really a good man, and everyone felt good about Him when He healed the sick and taught interesting parables. That's the kind of Jesus I want to embrace.*

But you must go far beyond that. To embrace Jesus by saving faith and enter His Kingdom, you must allow Him to expose your sin. That means you repent of your evil thoughts and deeds, come to Him for forgiveness, receive His justification, and begin to live a holy life. But if you hate Jesus for exposing your sin and refuse to repent, you'll die in your sins and go to hell. So Christ's life was and is a revelation. How people respond reveals the condition of their hearts.

The word Simeon used for "thoughts" in verse 35 connotes negative beliefs. He was indicating that Jesus would reveal the filth of sinful thoughts. Even the Son of God couldn't have a ministry as He did and still make everyone feel good all the time. As we have seen, He created such hostility that the people killed Him. When one represents and teaches the truth of holiness, as Christ did, he exposes the evil of the human heart.

Some people today, as in Jesus' time, will fall on their faces, repent, and believe. But many other people today, also as in Jesus' time, will reject Him and refuse to believe.

In summary, Simeon's testimony to Christ had far-reaching implications. Above all, it demonstrated the supreme joy of a righteous Jew whom God had allowed to meet the Messiah. The hope of Israel and the world was then realized—even though heartache and difficulty would result during the course of Jesus' ministry. Salvation had come, and Simeon could die in peace. His task, though brief and contained in a small segment of Scripture, was of great significance. God used Simeon to give a powerful affirmation to the truth that the infant Jesus was the promised Christ.

11

The Superiority of Jesus Christ

Chapter Eleven

❧

The Superiority of Jesus Christ

T HE TRUE CHRISTIAN should never take the story of Christ's birth for granted. Even when reread from the human perspective, the narrative of Christ's entrance into this world ought to remain forever fresh, fascinating, and awe-inspiring. There's the amazing appearance of the angel Gabriel to Mary to announce that she would bear God's Son. There's the intriguing interaction between Mary and Elizabeth (with a Spirit-inspired response from the unborn John the Baptist) as Mary sought confirmation of Gabriel's news. Then there is the unprecedented account of the angels' nighttime appearance to the shepherds right after Jesus was born. And finally, there are the varied and profound human responses to the significance of Christ's birth, from the divinely directed mission of the wise men to Simeon's Spirit-filled pronouncement at the temple.

All those events, as uplifting as we've found them in our study of the Incarnation, come only from the human perspective. But there is another absolutely essential viewpoint of Christ's birth that we must not omit—God's perspective. And you find that perspective in the New Testament Epistles. When the inspired writers of those letters look back to the birth of Jesus Christ, all they discuss is the person of Christ, which is very fitting because in the Gospel narratives there is no in-depth description or explanation of the Child Himself. There is not even a description of His physical appearance that would distinguish Him as divine rather than human. But the Epistles continually look back at the birth and life of Christ from God's perspective. They go beyond the human perspective of a baby in the manger to the divine perspective of His person and work.

For instance, Romans 1 asserts that Jesus was both the Son of David and the Son of God. Galatians 4:4 says that in the fullness of time God brought forth His Son, born of a woman and subject to the Law. Ephesians 3 introduces the concept of the mystery of Christ, that God has now revealed the truth of His Son in human flesh to the Jews *and* the Gentiles (cf. 1 Tim. 3). Philippians 2 teaches us that Christ during His Incarnation laid aside the form of deity and took on the form of humanity to die on the cross. Colossians 2 makes the sweeping and profound statement that the fullness of the Godhead dwelt bodily in Jesus Christ. But there is one other crowning passage among those that provides divine insight into the person of Jesus Christ—Hebrews 1. I believe that it is particularly important to understand this passage if we would have a complete grasp of the significance of Christ's birth.

A BRIEF INTRODUCTION TO HEBREWS

The letter to the Hebrews, written about A.D. 67–69 by an unidentified author, was obviously written to Jews, mostly true believers in Jesus. Its purpose was to show them that Jesus Christ is in fact the fulfillment of all the Old Testament Messianic promises and that He is superior to all the pictures, types, representations, and shadows that preceded Him. The Epistle was written to assure believing Jews that their faith was rightly placed and to encourage unbelieving Jews that embracing Jesus was the right commitment to make. Many in the community were intellectually convinced Jesus was the Messiah and God, but they had not yet personally believed and publicly confessed Him as Lord. They didn't want to be alienated like their believing friends had been. Some had been put out of the synagogue, some had been ostracized by their families, and others had lost their jobs.

In view of those fears and uncertainties, the writer of Hebrews wanted to encourage the Jews that in the long run they were not losing anything by embracing Jesus and confessing Him as Lord. The things they might have to give up in this life were worth it compared to what they would gain in full atonement for their sins and complete access to the very presence of God forever. So the writer affirms that the Babe born in Bethlehem is the Messiah and that He is indeed the Lord of a New Covenant, which is far superior to the Old Covenant of Moses.

Hebrews 1:1–3 launches right into the purpose of the Epistle: "God, who at various times and in various ways spoke in time past to the fathers by the prophets, has in these last days spoken to us by His Son, whom He has appointed heir of all things, through whom also He made the worlds; who being the brightness of His glory and the express image of His person, and upholding all things by the word of His power, when He had by Himself purged our sins, sat down at the right hand of the Majesty on high."

Here again in a few short verses is an insightful, divine description of who the baby born in Bethlehem really is. It is probably the most concise and comprehensive New Testament summary statement of the superiority of Christ. And the writer includes three key features in composing his classic statement: the preparation for Christ, the presentation of Christ, and the preeminence of Christ.

THE PREPARATION FOR CHRIST

Hebrews 1:1 refers to the Old Testament as it focuses on the preparation for Christ: "God, who at various times and in various ways spoke in time past to the fathers by the prophets." The Old Testament was simply God speaking to the Jewish people ("the fathers") through the prophets in many different ways and at a number of different times.

The prophets were men who spoke for God, and they did so "at various times," which actually means "portions" (NASB) or "segments." In other words, God's Spirit spoke through the Old Testament writers in thirty-nine different books. And these books come to us in various literary forms: Much of the literature is narrative prose and history, much is prophecy, some is poetry, and a little appears as the Law.

Furthermore, God's servants received His words "in various ways," or by different methods. Sometimes He spoke to them directly in audible words. At other times He spoke to them indirectly and prompted their minds with the thoughts He wanted conveyed. Then there were other methods by which God communicated His truth—parables, types, symbols, ceremonies, and even stone tablets (the Ten Commandments). But all of it was inspired, inerrant, and truly what God wanted written, the way He wanted it written.

The Old Testament is basically progressive revelation; it moves from a lesser degree of completeness to a fuller degree of completeness. It begins with what the apostle Paul later called the basic elements (Gal. 4:3, 9; Col. 2:8, 20), the early rules and regulations under the Law. Then it spells things out in greater detail through types and ceremonies. Finally, the prophetic books develop a more complete understanding of God's redemptive program (1 Pet. 1:10–12).

The writer of Hebrews and other New Testament writers recognized that all those features of the Old Testament affirmed its divine character. When Paul wrote, "All Scripture is given by inspiration of God" (2 Tim. 3:16), he was referring to the Old Testament. And when Peter said, "No prophecy of Scripture is of any private interpretation . . . but holy men of God spoke as they were moved by the Holy Spirit" (2 Pet. 1:20–21), he too was talking about the Old Testament.

And by affirming its features and character, the writer of Hebrews shows that the Old Testament is the preparation for Christ, because he also knew that its theme was Jesus Christ. From Genesis 3:15 (the first allusion to Christ and the gospel) to Malachi 4:1–3 (a reference to Christ's returning in judgment against the ungodly), the Lord Jesus is the subject all the way through the Old Testament. He's the One pictured in the sacrifices and ceremonies detailed in the five books of Moses. He's the great Prophet and King who's promised time and again (Num.

24:17; Deut. 18:15. 18; Ps. 2:6; 24:7–10; 45:6; 89:27; Isa. 9:7; 32:1; 42:1–2; 52:7; 61:1; Jer. 23:5; Dan. 7:14; Mic. 5:2; Zech. 9:9).

However, the Old Testament preparation for Christ is incomplete and fragmentary. Not one of its books or writers presents the entire picture of the Savior. We get only a partial view here and a partial insight there—and the inspired writers present those over a fifteen-hundred-year period. As the apostle Peter says, "Of this salvation the prophets have inquired and searched carefully, who prophesied of the grace that would come to you, searching what, or what manner of time, the Spirit of Christ who was in them was indicating when He testified beforehand the sufferings of Christ and the glories that would follow" (1 Pet. 1:10–11). The prophets couldn't sort everything out; they wondered exactly whom they were writing about and precisely when everything would occur.

The Old Testament's progressive revelation prepared its readers for the coming of Christ. But no one saw a complete picture of the Messiah until He actually came in the New Testament.

THE PRESENTATION OF CHRIST

The writer of Hebrews affirms that Christ is the full revelation of God when he says that God "has in these last days spoken to us by His Son" (1:2). When Jesus came, God presented the entire picture. Christ revealed God fully by being fully God. "For in Him [Christ] dwells all the fullness of the Godhead bodily" (Col. 2:9).

We can see in Christ everything we need to know about God. That includes the full array of God's attributes—such characteristics as omniscience, miracle-working power, the ability to heal the sick and raise the dead, compassion for sinners, and the desire for justice and holiness.

And all of that was evident "in these last days," a familiar phrase the Jews would have understood as meaning the Messianic age. Thus, in the time of Messiah, God ceased speaking in fragments and instead presented His complete revelation in the person of His Son. That, of course, established Jesus as superior to previous revelation. The incomplete Old Testament issued from the prophets, who were sinful men. In contrast, the complete and final New Testament came forth in the person of the sinless Son of God. Jesus Christ, as the full expression of His Father, could say, "'He who has seen Me has seen the Father'" (John 14:9).

THE PREEMINENCE OF CHRIST

Once the writer of Hebrews presents Jesus as God's Son, he immediately gives us a sevenfold summary of the preeminence of Jesus Christ: "whom He has appointed heir of all things, through whom also He made the worlds; who being the brightness of His glory and the express image of His person, and upholding all things by the word of His power, when He had by Himself purged our sins, sat down at the right hand of the Majesty on high" (1:2–3). That is the grand summation and definitive listing of the characteristics that really identify the Child who entered the world at Bethlehem. Anyone who truly confesses Jesus as Lord and Savior affirms the truth of each of those elements. That's why it's important to take a brief look at each one.

Christ Is the Heir of All Things

The first aspect of Jesus Christ's preeminence concerns His inheritance: "whom He has appointed heir of all things." That is an unqualified statement asserting that God has planned for Jesus ultimately to inherit absolutely everything. It adheres to Jewish inheritance laws that said the firstborn child received the wealth of the family's estate.

Because Jesus is the only begotten Son of God, He is logically the firstborn Son as well. Therefore, Christ is the heir of all that God has. The psalmist predicted this very reality, "I [God] will give You the nations for Your inheritance, and the ends of the earth for Your possession" (Ps. 2:8). Everything in the created order, whether the material or spiritual world— everything God has ever created—belongs to Jesus Christ.

It's amazing to think that a Galilean carpenter, crucified on a cross outside Jerusalem, is actually the heir to the universe. Admittedly, when Jesus was on earth He owned little or nothing. One thing He did own was His cloak, and the Roman soldiers gambled for ownership of that while He was on the cross. He was even buried in a borrowed grave. But some day, all that exists will belong to Christ, and everyone—people, angels, and all powers in the universe—will bow before Him. "At the name of Jesus every knee should bow, of those in heaven, and of those on earth, and of those under the earth" (Phil. 2:10).

It's also incredible to realize that believers will be joint heirs with Christ: "The Spirit Himself bears witness with our spirit that we are children of God, and if children, then heirs—heirs of God and joint heirs with Christ" (Rom. 8:16–17). If you know Christ, you are a part of His bride, the church, and He, the Bridegroom, allows you to share His inheritance. And someday you will see Him return as King of kings and Lord of lords to make final claim of His inheritance and exercise sovereign, everlasting rule over all that exists. Therefore, once you say Jesus is Lord, you also say He is the heir of all things.

Christ Is the Agent of Creation

The second preeminence of Christ listed in Hebrews 1 is His power in creation: "through whom also He made the worlds" (v. 2). That statement is perfectly consistent with John 1:3, "All things were made through Him, and without Him nothing was made that was made" (Col. 1:16; Heb. 11:3). Jesus created everything, both the material and nonmaterial parts of the universe. And His creatorship is a characteristic of our Lord—second only to His sinlessness—that really sets Him apart from us.

The Greek word rendered "worlds" in Hebrews 1:2 does not mean the material world but "the ages," as it is usually translated elsewhere. Christ created not only the physical earth, but also time, space, energy, and every variety of matter. He effortlessly created the entire universe and finished it as something good. For that reason the creation, which was marred by humanity's sin, longs to be restored to what it was originally (Rom.

8:22)—and one day Christ will create a new and perfect heaven and earth.

Christ Possesses the Brightness of God's Glory

The writer of Hebrews further establishes the preeminence of Christ by citing that He is "the brightness of His [God's] glory." "Brightness," which may also be translated "radiance" (NASB) and literally means "to send forth light," indicates that Jesus is the manifestation of God to us. Just as the sun's rays illuminate and warm the earth, Christ is God's glorious light that shines into the hearts of people. And as the sun cannot be separated from its brightness, so God cannot be separated from the glory of Christ. Yet the brightness of the sun is not the sun, and in the same sense, neither is the brightness of Christ God. That does not mean that Christ is not fully and absolutely God. It simply means the Son of God is a distinct person within the Godhead.

Jesus Christ is the radiance of who God is, and He affirmed that fact during His earthly ministry: "'I am the light of the world. He who follows Me shall not walk in darkness, but have the light of life'" (John 8:12). Christ can transmit that light into our lives so that we can radiate the glory of God to others. God sent His glorious light, in the person of Jesus Christ, into a morally dark world to call sinners to Himself. No one would ever be able to see or enjoy God's true radiance if it weren't for His Son and those who know Him.

It is truly a blessing to know that Jesus Christ can come into your life and give you the spiritual light to see and believe God. Jesus' brightness points you to salvation, which in turn results in purpose, peace, joy, and genuine fellowship for all eternity.

Christ Is the Essence of God

Hebrews 1:3 goes on to declare a fourth element of the preeminence of Christ, namely, "the express image of His person." Jesus possesses the essential nature or being of God the Father. That is, He has all the attributes that are indispensable to who and what God is, such as immutability (unchangeableness), omniscience, omnipotence, and omnipresence. He is the exact stamp or replication of God. In the words of the Nicene Creed, Jesus Christ is "very God of very God."

The apostle Paul teaches us basically the same truth in Colossians 1:15, "He is the image of the invisible God." Here, unlike Hebrews 1:3, the Greek word translated "image" is *eikon,* from which we get the English term *icon,* meaning a precise copy or reproduction. But both verses communicate the same truth. Christ possesses the essential nature of God and manifests the communicable attributes of God. In His being, Jesus is what God is, and in His person He displays that essence to everyone who sees Him.

Whenever people talk about the baby in the manger, they are talking about none other than God.

Christ Has Ultimate Authority

Fifth in the list of Christ's preeminent qualities is that He has always been "upholding all things by the word of His power" (Heb. 1:3). As we have already seen, He is the Creator of the entire universe, material and nonmaterial. But Christ's authority does not stop there. He upholds and sustains all that He has created.

Christ follows the principle of cohesion; He makes the universe a cosmos instead of chaos. He infallibly ensures that the universe runs as an ordered, reliable unit instead of as an erratic, unpredictable muddle. That's because our Lord has devised and implemented the myriad natural laws, both complex and straightforward, that are all perfectly reliable, consistent, and precisely suited to their particular purposes. Time and again they wonderfully demonstrate the mind and power of Jesus Christ working through the universe.

No scientist, mathematician, astronomer, or nuclear physicist could do anything or discover anything apart from the sustaining power and authority of Christ. The whole universe hangs on His powerful arm, His infinite wisdom, and His ability to control every element and orchestrate the movements of every molecule, atom, and subatomic particle.

For example, if the size of the earth's orbit around the sun increased or decreased even the slightest amount, we would soon fatally freeze or fry. If the earth's angle of tilt went beyond its present range even slightly, that would drastically disrupt the familiar four-season cycle and threaten to end life on the planet. Similarly, if the moon's orbit around the earth diminished, the ocean tides would greatly increase and cause unimaginable havoc. And if our atmosphere thinned just a little, many of the thousands of meteors that now enter it and harmlessly incinerate before striking the ground would crash to the surface with potentially catastrophic results.

Jesus Christ prevents such disasters by perfectly maintaining the universe's intricate balance. The most astronomical distances and largest objects are not beyond His control. The most delicate and microscopic processes do not escape His attention. He is the preeminent power and authority who nevertheless came to earth in human form, assuming a servant's role.

Christ Removes Our Sins

The sixth aspect of Christ's preeminence deals directly with our salvation. Hebrews 1:3 expresses it this way, "He had by Himself purged our sins." Jesus, by His atoning death, brought about the purging or cleansing of our sins. That is what we needed most, and only the Lord Jesus could meet the need.

The Old Testament priests offered animal sacrifices over and over, but none of those could ultimately remove the people's sins. Those repeated sacrifices instead merely pointed to the desperate need for a once-for-all sacrifice that could finally take away sins. And God provided such a sacrifice in the person of Jesus. As the writer of Hebrews later wrote, "So Christ was offered once to bear the sins of many" (9:28); "for by one offering He has perfected forever those who are being sanctified" (10:14).

In keeping with the Old Testament Law that the sacrificial lamb had to be spotless, the final New Covenant sacrifice had to be a perfect, sinless substitute. To pay the price of sin for others, he had to be perfect or he would have had to pay the price for his own sin. And since no one in the world is without sin, the substitute had to be someone from outside the world. Yet he still needed to be a man to die in the place of men and women.

Of course, the only person who could meet those requirements was Jesus Christ. He was the sinless man who could be the perfect substitute for sinners. By offering Himself to die on the cross, He took the full wrath of God for sinners like you and me. That wrath, which was originally directed toward us, was then satisfied. Thus God can forgive you because Christ paid the penalty for your sin.

So one of the preeminent glories of Christ is that, as the God-Man, He came to die for sinners. And He died on the cross to accomplish redemption. Immediately prior to His death, Jesus uttered these profound words, "'It is finished!'" (John 19:30); once and for all He paid the price for sins for everyone who would ever believe in Him.

Christ Is Exalted in Heaven

The author concludes his marvelous outline of the preeminence of Christ by affirming His exaltation: "[He] sat down at the right hand of the Majesty on high" (1:3).

Christ's ministry on earth ended forty days after His resurrection when He ascended into heaven (Acts 1:9–11). And when He returned there, God seated Him at His right hand (Ps. 110:1; Heb. 1:13; 8:1; 10:12; 12:2), which always symbolized the side of power, authority, prominence, and preeminence (Rom. 8:34; 1 Pet. 3:22). Paul says that at that point God gave Him a name above all names—"Lord," which is the New Testament synonym for Old Testament descriptions of God as sovereign ruler (Phil. 2:9–11).

When Jesus went into heaven, He did what no Old Testament priest ever did—He sat down. They never sat down while ministering because their work was never done. But Christ's work was done; He had accomplished the work of redemption on the Cross, and therefore it was appropriate for Him to sit down. He remains on the right hand of the throne of God as the believer's great High Priest and Intercessor (Heb. 7:25; 9:24).

JESUS CHRIST IS SUPERIOR TO THE ANGELS

The writer of Hebrews hardly needed to tell his Jewish readers any more concerning the magnificent preeminence of Christ. But just to underscore the truth of Jesus' supremacy, the writer sets forth another persuasive point—this one more expansive than the others—beginning in 1:4–5, "Having become so much better than the angels, as He has by inheritance obtained a more excellent name than they. For to which of the angels did He ever say: 'You are My Son, today I have begotten You'?"

At Bethlehem the night of Jesus' birth, the heavenly host that appeared above the shepherds' field might have been more impressive than a humble Child wrapped in cloths and lying in a feed trough. Such a baby was not recognizable as God, but He was God nonetheless and therefore superior to any array of angels. And that's what the writer sought to convince the Jews of as he contrasted Christ to the angels.

Jewish Beliefs Concerning Angels

The Jews in biblical times greatly esteemed angels. Every devout Jew knew about the angels' important role in God's unfolding purpose among humanity. The Jews believed angels surrounded God's throne and worshiped Him (Isaiah 6). They also believed angels were messengers who did God's work and occasionally came to earth to mediate between God and mankind, as occurred with Abraham and Lot (Gen. 18:1–19:29) and Daniel (Dan. 8:15–27).

But most important, the Jews believed angels were the divinely sent agents who delivered the Old Covenant, the Mosaic Law. They knew the Law was a holy and righteous reflection of God's will, and they tried to live by it (which meant, unfortunately, that many of them saw the Law as their means of salvation).

So the Jews had great reverence for angels. In fact, they had so much respect that they revered no one but God more.

With that in mind, the writer of Hebrews argues that Jesus has a much better and more excellent name than the angels. "For to which of the angels did He ever say: 'You are My Son, today I have begotten You'?" (1:5). The answer to that rhetorical question is quite obviously, "None." So if Jesus had that kind of advantage over all the angels, the Jews had to infer His superiority; and they knew that if anyone is superior to the angels, he has to be God.

How Is Christ Superior to the Angels?

Because serious-minded Jews had such great reverence and respect for the position of angels and the place of the Old Testament, the writer worked extra diligently to nail down his argument concerning Christ's superiority. It was essential for his Jewish readers to see that Messiah is better than the bearers and mediators of the Old Testament. The author establishes that point by concluding chapter 1 with an effective use of seven Old Testament passages.

If he had tried to prove his case from Christian writings, his audience could easily have said, "We don't accept those documents as coming from God; therefore, we reject your argument." So he wisely and skillfully demonstrated directly from key Old Testament verses five ways that Christ is superior to the angels.

First of all, Jesus is superior *by virtue of His name*. We've already had a glimpse of this truth in 1:4, "Having become so much better than the angels, as He has by inheritance obtained a more excellent name than they." Jesus has a better name because He has inherited it from God the Father. He can make a legitimate claim to that better name because of

His essential nature, as verse 5 says, "For to which of the angels did He ever say: "'You are My Son, today I have begotten You'?" Generally, angels and people are sons of God simply because God created them. But He never told a single one of the angels that he was a son who proceeded from Him. He reserved that designation for Christ alone.

By saying, "You are My Son," God revealed that Jesus shared the same essence as the Father. And the Jews would understand that to mean that Jesus possessed precisely the same characteristics as God the Father.

In spite of the Jews' unbelief and doubts—in the Book of Hebrews and prior—Jesus was and is the Son of God. God gave Him the name "Son," which expresses Christ's eternal generation from the Father. There never was a moment in all of eternity when the Son did not exist. In a way we can't fully grasp, the Father-Son relationship expresses a shared divine nature and an equal inheritance to all that exists in the universe. Angels are merely called messengers of God, but Jesus is called the Son of God: "And again: 'I will be to Him a Father, and He shall be to Me a Son'" (Heb. 1:5).

Second, Jesus is superior to the angels *because of His rank:* "But when He again brings the firstborn into the world, He says: 'Let all the angels of God worship Him'" (Heb. 1:6).

The Greek word for "firstborn" is not a word of chronology or birth sequence; it's a word of preeminence. More clearly rendered, it would read "the preeminent one, the prominent one, the highest one." Because there is only one Son of God, it was not necessary for the writer to distinguish the firstborn Son from the second or third Son.

"Firstborn" also does not mean Jesus is the preeminent member of the Trinity or that He is the highest ranking in some procession of deities from God's throne. Rather, it means He is the supreme One over all creation (Col. 1:15). The writer of Hebrews supports this truth by quoting the Greek Old Testament translation of Deuteronomy 32:43, which itself relates to Psalm 89:6. That's where the psalmist says the angels must recognize God's lordship. The angels are created beings, and Christ as Creator is superior to them. And so they are commanded, as a primary function of their position, to worship and serve Him, the superior One (Ps. 89:27; 97:7).

Jesus is also superior to the angels *because of His essential nature.* The author of Hebrews, again drawing from the Old Testament (first Psalm 104:4; then Psalm 45:6–7; then Isaiah 61:1, 3), compares Christ's nature to the angels': "And of the angels He says: 'Who makes His angels spirits and His ministers a flame of fire.' But to the Son He says: 'Your throne, O God, is forever and ever; a scepter of righteousness is the scepter of Your kingdom. You have loved righteousness and hated lawlessness; therefore God, Your God, has anointed You with the oil of gladness more than Your companions'" (Heb. 1:7–9).

The angels are created spirit beings, described metaphorically in these verses as a collective flame of fire. But in contrast, Christ the Son is eternal God. That is the basic distinction—the angels are created; Christ is eternal.

The writer indicates the difference first by mentioning God the Son's eternal throne and then describing how He rules. Righteousness, depicted as "a scepter of righteousness," is the chief characteristic of His reign. That means the Lord Jesus loves righteousness and hates lawlessness, which are simply two primary aspects of the same divine holiness.

But as created beings, not all the angels chose to love righteousness and hate lawlessness. Initially angels were not impeccable, which means they had the capacity to sin and did so when a third of them followed Lucifer's rebellion against God. God expelled them and Lucifer (now Satan) from heaven, and today they are demons serving the dark purposes of the devil's kingdom.

However, the eternal Son of God has forever loved righteousness and hated lawlessness. It was impossible for Him to fall into sin. And that's the fundamental difference in His nature that sets Him far above even the holy angels and believing humanity. The conclusion of Hebrews 1:9 wonderfully portrays Christ's superior nature: "therefore God, Your God, has anointed You with the oil of gladness more than Your companions."

The writer continues to quote the Old Testament as he proclaims a fourth way Jesus is equal with God and exalted above the angels. *Christ possesses eternality*—He was and is God forever—a truth verified by reference to Psalm 102:25–27, "'You, Lord, in the beginning laid the foundation of the earth, and the heavens are the work of Your hands. They will perish, but You remain; and they will all grow old like a garment; like a cloak You will fold them up, and they will be changed. But You are the same, and your years will not fail'" (Hebrews 1:10–12).

The writer of Hebrews views Jesus as present at the creation because He was the Creator (John 1:3). Therefore His eternality stretches not only into the infinite past, but also into the infinite future. But that is not true concerning the universe. Someday Christ will "uncreate" an aging creation. He will fold up the heavens and the earth and replace them with something new. However, the Son of God never changes. "Jesus Christ is the same yesterday, today, and forever" (Heb. 13:8).

Finally, Christ is God and superior to the angels *by virtue of His destiny.* The writer again turns to the Psalms (110:1) and asks his Jewish audience, "But to which of the angels has He ever said: 'Sit at My right hand, till I make Your enemies Your footstool'?" (Hebrews 1:13). God never promised any of the angels that kind of ultimate, eternal sovereignty. But it is the destiny of Jesus Christ to rule over all, especially over those who know Him. The apostle John later wrote, "And I heard, as it were, the voice of a great multitude, as the sound of many waters and as the sound of mighty thunderings, saying, 'Alleluia! For the Lord God Omnipotent reigns! Let us be glad and rejoice and give Him glory, for the marriage of the Lamb has come'" (Rev. 19:6–7).

Hebrews 1:14 makes this final distinction between Christ and the angels completely clear: "Are they not all ministering spirits sent forth to minister for those who will inherit salvation?" Unlike Jesus, the angels aren't sovereign rulers; they're ministering servants, subject to His commands.

We don't see them, but God dispatches His angels for the protection and care of believers on earth (Matt. 18:10). And beyond that, the future tense ("will inherit") looks ahead to the full inheritance of our salvation and what the angels will continue to do for us. In the glories of heaven the Son will reign over us and we will worship Him as our King (Rom. 8:16–17; Eph. 1:11; Col. 1:12; 3:24). But amazingly, the angels will continue to serve us. Thus God created the angels to serve Christ's church in both time and eternity. And that underscores once again the angels' subordination to the Son of God.

When you read and study Hebrews 1, the wonderful truth of Jesus Christ's preeminence and superiority shines forth from every verse. You can't miss it, whether it's in His inheritance of all things, His agency in creation, His essential nature as God, His atoning death for sinners, or the various ways in which He is superior to the angels. The entire chapter effectively proclaims the Messiah's true identity and rightful position.

I believe an analysis of Hebrews 1:1–14 is a fitting capstone to a book on the birth of Christ. It ensures that when you consider the baby in the Bethlehem shelter, you don't merely see an adorable child who grew up to be a good teacher and compassionate healer. The passage points you beyond that and to an accurate understanding of the person and work of Christ. The writer, through careful, Spirit-inspired argumentation, declares irrefutably that the Child born to Mary was indeed God in the manger. He truly was the Son of God, miraculously conceived by the Holy Spirit yet born naturally to a woman in Israel. And without doubt He was the Lord and Savior who lived a perfect life and died as a perfect sacrifice so that all who believe in Him might have eternal life.

Study Guide

CHAPTER 1
THE AMAZING FACT OF THE VIRGIN BIRTH

Summarizing the Chapter

Matthew 1:18–25, with supporting reference to Isaiah 7:14, clearly sets forth the truth of Christ's virgin birth, which necessarily helps us make sense of His special birth, unique identity, and later earthly ministry.

Getting Started (Choose One)

1. Do you like mythology and fantasy stories? If so, what is your favorite one and why? If you don't like them, what are your main objections to those art forms and why?
2. Do you think it's appropriate to belong to an organization, association, club, or political party and not accept everything the group stands for? Have you ever tried to maintain such a membership? If so, what was the most difficult aspect?

ANSWERING THE QUESTIONS

1. Name three Old Testament characters whose births were extraordinary. What were the basic circumstances surrounding each birth?

2. How did pagan religions affect people's understanding of Christ's virgin birth? Illustrate the point by describing some of the specific unbiblical theories or myths about the birth of ancient pagan deities.

3. What has been the prevailing attitude toward Jesus' identity ever since the Fall? Why should that not discourage us?

4. What does the concise nature of Matthew 1:18 suggest about the doctrine of the virgin birth?

5. What were two standard characteristics of the Jewish betrothal in New Testament times?

6. Jesus' virgin birth ensures the credibility of what important doctrinal truths concerning His identity and ministry?

7. What twofold difficulty faced Joseph after he heard Mary was pregnant? What intensified the difficulty and made his response harder?

8. What did God do to spare Joseph from responding to Mary's pregnancy as he had initially planned?

9. How does the name Jesus define the purpose for God's Son coming to earth?

10. Was the idea of a virgin birth a completely new one to the Jews?

11. What passage gives the first glimpse that Christ's birth would be special?

12. What two events do the prophecy of Isaiah 7:14 refer to? What were they both signs of?

13. Why is it significant that Scripture uses 'alma and parthenos in Isaiah 7:14 and Matthew 1:23, respectively?

14. What references, implied and directly stated, prove that Mary was not a lifelong virgin?

FOCUSING ON PRAYER

- Thank the Lord for the truth and necessity of Jesus' virgin birth. Ask Him for the strength never to ignore or de-emphasize that doctrinal conviction.
- Pray for Joseph's type of faith and courage to do what's righteous in difficult circumstances.

APPLYING THE TRUTH

Choose one of the following to memorize: Isaiah 7:14; 1 Corinthians 13:12; Galatians 4:4. Memorize your verse in at least two different English versions.

CHAPTER 2
A LOOK AT JESUS' FAMILY TREE

SUMMARIZING THE CHAPTER

Christ's genealogy in Matthew and Luke is far more than two boring lists of Hebrew names that identify His paternal and maternal ancestors. Those lists, through their similarities and differences, help verify that Jesus was fully God and fully man.

Getting Started (Choose One)

1. Have you ever done any genealogical research to identify your ancestors? If not, why not? If so, what was the most interesting discovery you made?
2. How do you usually respond to lists of names as you're reading in the Old Testament? Do you read them carefully or skim over them? What does the relative frequency of such lists suggest about their importance?

ANSWERING THE QUESTIONS

1. What were the four major reasons genealogies were so important to the ancient Jews? Give a brief explanatory comment about each reason.

2. What two facts does the Gospel writers' use of Jesus' genealogical records demonstrate?

3. How does Luke's chronological view of Jesus' family tree differ from Matthew's? Which one presents a more dramatic tone to the chronology?

4. What are the main differences in names between the two lists?

5. What is the clearest, most obvious explanation for the existence of two different genealogies for Jesus?

6. What legal reason further required the recording of two *different* forms of Jesus' genealogy?

7. What potential charge against Jesus by His enemies never occurs in the Gospels? Why?

8. What is significant about the phrase, "being (as was supposed) the son of Joseph" (Luke 3:23)?

9. Why does Luke's genealogy use the term "son" only before Joseph's name?

10. In summary, what four important facts does Luke's genealogy assert that verify Jesus' divine credentials?

FOCUSING ON PRAYER

Praise and thank God that He guarded the accuracy of Christ's genealogy so we might have one more certain proof that Jesus is God's Son.

APPLYING THE TRUTH

Excluding the most well-known names such as David and Abraham, choose one or more familiar names from Jesus' genealogy and read more about the person in the Old Testament. Use tools such as a Bible dictionary, commentary, and study Bible to help you. What character traits or personal circumstances of the person remind you of Jesus? Which ones seem incongruous for an ancestor of Christ? Explain your answers, and share the main insights from your study with someone else.

CHAPTER 3
THE ANGEL'S ANNOUNCEMENT TO MARY

SUMMARIZING THE CHAPTER

The angel Gabriel's announcement to Mary that she was divinely chosen to bear God's Son, Jesus, the King of kings, Lord of lords, and Savior, was the most startling and far-reaching birth announcement in all of human history.

Getting Started (Choose One)

1. What extraordinary news announcement during your lifetime is most memorable to you? Why? How did you first hear about this news?
2. Do you enjoy having unexpected visits from friends or relatives? Would you say most people share your preference? Why or why not?

ANSWERING THE QUESTIONS

1. Approximately how many Old Testament prophesies and promises are there concerning the coming Messiah?
2. Why was it so amazing that God chose to send an angel to Mary?
3. Where else in Scripture did the angel Gabriel deliver an important message from heaven?

4. What was so remarkable about Galilee's role regarding the birth of Jesus?

5. What is the Hebrew equivalent of Mary and what does it mean?

6. . What was so astonishing about God's choice of Mary to bear His Son?

7. Why was Gabriel's first word to Mary so low-key?

8. What heresy does an accurate and complete reading of Luke 1:28 refute?

9. Why was Mary somewhat confused and perplexed when she heard Gabriel's greeting? What additional emotion defined her response?

10. At first, how did Mary likely think she would fulfill the angel's words about conceiving a son?

11. Name three references in Luke 2 that reiterate and underscore Gabriel's declaration that Jesus was indeed the promised Savior.

12. What synonyms for *great* could we use to describe Jesus' life? How was His greatness different from John the Baptist's?

13. In what ways is Jesus' title "Son of the Highest" significant?

14. What does the Bible promise all believers in regard to Christ's Kingdom?

FOCUSING ON PRAYER

• Ask the Lord to give you as much reverence and humility toward His commandments as Mary had.

• If you are a Christian, thank God that He extended His saving grace to you and made you a member of His Kingdom.

APPLYING THE TRUTH

Read and meditate on each of the following Old Testament passages that look ahead to Messiah: Genesis 3:15; 49:10; Deuteronomy 18:15; Psalm 2:6–12; Isaiah 9:6–7; 52:13–53:12; Daniel 2:45; 7:13–14; 9:26; Micah 5:2. Using a concordance and study Bible, do some additional study on a few important words and phrases from the passages. Write a short summary of how this exercise has been helpful to you and pray for opportunities to apply what you've learned.

CHAPTER 4
WILL THIS NEWS REALLY COME TRUE?

SUMMARIZING THE CHAPTER

Mary visited her older relative Elizabeth and received three confirmations—personal, physical, and prophetic—that she actually would become the mother of Jesus.

Getting Started (Choose One)

1. When you hear promises that involve you personally, is it hard for you to believe they will come true? Is there anything now that would fit this category? Describe the promise and explain why you are or are not struggling to accept its fulfillment.

2. What is the most encouraging word or good deed someone ever spoke or performed on your behalf? What were the circumstances and why was the experience so helpful? How often are you able to encourage others?

ANSWERING THE QUESTIONS

1. In Luke 1, how is the account of Mary's conception miracle similar to the earlier one involving Elizabeth? List at least four similarities.

2. What were three questions or factors that compelled Mary to visit her relative Elizabeth right away?

3. Why was Elizabeth the ideal person to confirm Gabriel's words to Mary?

4. What did the traditional Near Eastern greeting include (Exod. 18:7–9)?

5. How and why was John the Baptist's prenatal leap so significant? Was there any scriptural precedent for such activity? When?

6. What two general principles did Elizabeth's Spirit-filled, prophetic exclamation demonstrate?

7. Who are the four individuals or groups that Elizabeth's statement blessed?

8. How was Mary a model of faith for us?

FOCUSING ON PRAYER

• Pray for your pastor or another Christian leader you know. Ask God to grant Him encouragement and confirmation that his ministry is pleasing to the Lord and that his trust in God's will for his life is credible.

• Ask God for the grace and courage to follow Mary's example of faithful obedience in response to all His commands.

APPLYING THE TRUTH

Memorize John 3:29 or 2 Peter 1:20–21.

CHAPTER 5
A HUMBLE BIRTH IN BETHLEHEM

SUMMARIZING THE CHAPTER

God sovereignly orchestrated, through world and national circumstances, Joseph and Mary's visit to Bethlehem so that Jesus was born exactly according to divine plan.

1. We shouldn't dispute the fact that God is still involved in world events. But is that involvement as evident as it was before Christ was born? Explain your answer.

2. Have you ever had an unusual, humorous, or difficult experience involving hotel reservations? How did the Lord finally resolve the situation? What was the main lesson you learned from it?

ANSWERING THE QUESTIONS

1. Which Old Testament prophet predicted that Messiah would be born in Bethlehem? Why is it clear that his famous prophecy points to Christ and no other figure? ·

2. Why did the Jews particularly hate the Romans and their occupation of Israel?

3. What was Caesar Augustus' original name? Name two famous Roman leaders he had interaction with when he was a young man.

4. What was the significance of Augustus's Pax Romana?

5. What were the two reasons that Rome required census registrations?

6. Why did the Jews despise Roman taxes so much? What was God's true reason for scheduling the tax registration prior to Jesus' birth?

7. What two pagan Old Testament-era rulers parallel Augustus in the way God used them?

8. What requirement concerning the tax registration did the Romans change to accommodate Joseph and Mary and other Jews?

9. List the various towns, significant since Old Testament times, that Joseph and Mary likely would have passed through on their way from Nazareth to Bethlehem.

10. What reference first affirms Bethlehem as David's city? Name one or two other passages that support this fact.

11. What does the term "inn" in Luke 2:7 really denote? How does that help explain where Mary and Joseph actually stayed when Jesus was born?

12. In what ways was the expression "firstborn Son" important in explaining the uniqueness of Christ's birth and the kind of rights and privileges He had as a son?

13. What was Luke's primary point in mentioning Mary's use of "swaddling cloths"?

14. What's a more literal translation for "manger" (Luke 2:7)? How does that meaning sharpen the picture even further regarding where the baby Jesus and His parents were staying?

FOCUSING ON PRAYER

- Thank the Lord that He providentially worked in such wonderful ways to ensure that Christ's birth occurred exactly according to divine plan. And thank Him that He is still in control of world events today.

- Pray that the picture of God's grace, portrayed so well by Christ's willingness to be born in a smelly, uncomfortable shelter, would be instrumental in an unsaved friend or relative's seeing beyond a familiar Christmas story and realizing their need for salvation.

APPLYING THE TRUTH

In your own words, write an expanded version of Luke 2:1–7. Use some of the facts contained in chapter 5 to flesh out and amplify Luke's original sentences. Conclude with a summary statement that captures the historical and doctrinal significance of the passage. Share your paraphrase with someone and tell him or her how writing it helped you mentally solidify and better appreciate the truths of Luke's account.

CHAPTER 6
THE HEAVENLY ANNOUNCEMENT OF JESUS' BIRTH

Summarizing the Chapter

The angels' announcement of Jesus' birth was the high point of redemptive history because it was nothing less than a supernatural proclamation of the gospel, which emphasized the nature and scope of the good news.

Getting Started (Choose One)

1. Would you consider the town you were born in small and obscure? If not, do you ever wish it had been? Why or why not? How do you think the area in which you lived shaped your early life?
2. What segment or class of people in your culture do you think is most underappreciated? How do you believe they could be more respected? Why is that and how do you think it would make a difference?

Answering the Questions

1. In making His first announcement of Christ's birth to the shepherds, what Old Testament prophecy did God help fulfill?
2. What prominent Bible characters were shepherds at one time or another? What notion does that tend to disprove about the nature of shepherding?
3. In Jewish social and religious circles, why and how were shepherds despised as outcasts?
4. The appearance to the shepherds emphasized what important salvation truth?
5. What is the simple definition of "the glory of the Lord"? Give two Old Testament examples of this.
6. What other Scripture examples would you use to illustrate that the

shepherds' fear in the presence of God's glory was not unprecedented?

7. Did the shepherds really need to be afraid? Why or why not? What other kind of fear would they have understood as appropriate and necessary?

8. What familiar English words derive from "I bring you good tidings" (Luke 2:10)?

9. How can the pervasiveness of the gospel have both a worldwide and individual aspect? Briefly explain each and cite several key Bible passages.

10. What does the term "Christ" mean and why is it so remarkable that the infant Jesus would bear that title?

11. What threefold basis did God the Father have for proclaiming Jesus the Christ? Provide a Scripture reference to support each of the three aspects.

12. What two major truths does the phrase "Jesus is Lord" reveal about Him? What Old Testament prophet foresaw this meaning when he uttered a well-known prophecy?

13. What is the basic purpose of the gospel? What ultimate purpose does that support?

14. What familiar statement summarizes the angelic host's entire praise to God (Luke 2:14)? Each of its final two phrases has long been misinterpreted. Explain how for each one. What is the accurate meaning of each?

FOCUSING ON PRAYER

- Pray that the Lord would grant you the same kind of humility and faith that the shepherds displayed.
- Thank God for the essential truths contained in the gospel, and ask Him that He would seal them to you with a greater-than-ever depth of understanding. Pray that, as a result, you would be a more effective witness.

APPLYING THE TRUTH

During the upcoming month, seek to memorize three passages that speak of Jesus' Messianic office: Prophet (Heb. 1:1–2), High Priest (1 Tim. 2:5), and King (John 18:37). Choose one for additional meditation and in-depth study.

CHAPTER 7
THE TESTIMONY OF SHEPHERDS

SUMMARIZING THE CHAPTER

The shepherds' response of faith and obedience to what they saw and heard from the angels is an excellent illustration of the Christian life: You hear and believe the gospel, you embrace Christ, you tell others about Him, and you go on to live the rest of your life in obedience to Him.

Getting Started (Choose One)

1. What's the most spectacular sight or event you've ever seen? Explain why you chose it. Has witnessing it had any long-term effect on your thoughts or actions? If so, how?

2. Is it easy or hard for you to find your way around an unfamiliar city or neighborhood? Do you tend to ask for directions right away when you're lost, or do you keep on looking for your destination? What is the most rewarding or frustrating experience you've ever had in exploring a new community?

ANSWERING THE QUESTIONS

1. How long did the heavenly host probably remain before the shepherds?

2. What kind of response did the shepherds have immediately after the angels departed?

3. The shepherds wanted to "see this thing that has happened." What does the Greek for "thing" connote that is not so apparent in English? How could the "thing" be verified?

4. In what manner did the shepherds proceed as they sought Jesus in Bethlehem? Elaborate briefly.

5. What was striking about the experiences the shepherds and Jesus' parents shared around the manger?

6. What kind of general reaction have people always tended to have to Jesus? Why is that reaction not necessarily sufficient?

7. What sorts of questions did Mary likely ask as she pondered all the events surrounding Christ's birth?

8. How should Mary's response and thoughts parallel the mature believer's Christian experience?

9. Why would Mary and Joseph have brought Jesus for circumcision? Did He, as the Son of God, really need to undergo this procedure? Why?

FOCUSING ON PRAYER

- Ask the Lord for the same eagerness and enthusiasm in obeying God's commands as the shepherds had.

- Thank and praise God that Mary wanted to please God and that she and Joseph were faithful parents who helped Jesus obey God's requirements even when their son was an infant.

APPLYING THE TRUTH

Perhaps you have been praying for the salvation of a friend or relative. Arrange to visit the person, with the goal in mind of sharing the gospel with him or her. If you can't make a personal visit, consider writing an evangelistic letter to the person and enclosing a God-centered tract with your letter.

If at this time you have no unsaved friend or relative to visit, ask the Lord for a good opportunity to share with another believer something significant you have learned recently in your walk with Christ.

CHAPTER 8
THE NEWS TRAVELS FAST

SUMMARIZING THE CHAPTER

The three different responses to Christ's birth—the Magi's worship, Herod's hostility, and the Jewish leaders' indifference—reflect the basic reactions to Jesus Christ that people have demonstrated throughout history.

GETTING STARTED (CHOOSE ONE)

1. In Christmas pageants you saw or participated in while growing up, how were the wise men portrayed? Based on your current understanding, were those depictions accurate? Discuss.
2. Do people's motives—even believers'—in Christmas gift giving measure up to the attitude implicit in the Magi's gift giving to Jesus? What do you think would improve today's custom of exchanging gifts? What, if anything, do you appreciate most about that Christmas tradition?

ANSWERING THE QUESTIONS

1. What sorts of myths and erroneous traditions have distorted people's understanding of the Magi narrative?
2. When and where did Magi originate? What were some of their major distinctives?
3. What basic trait characterized the Magi who sought Jesus? Name two like-minded Gentiles whom the New Testament mentions later on.

4. What have people conjectured about the identity of the star in the East? List at least three speculations.

5. What is the most plausible and probably most biblical explanation to identify the star?

6. What idea does the Greek for "worship" express? What does that indicate regarding the identity of the wise men?

7. What character traits was Herod the Great known for? How successful was he as a leader before he returned to Palestine as "king of the Jews"?

8. What ethnicity was Herod? Did that prevent him from being familiar with Jewish customs and beliefs?

9. What action did Herod order when the Magi did not report back to him? What did that reveal about his true desire concerning Jesus?

10. What groups constituted the Jewish leaders that Herod summoned to learn more about Christ's birthplace? Briefly describe each group.

11. How did the Jewish leaders' intellectual knowledge of God's Messianic promises benefit them? What more did those men need to do with that awareness? Where did they end up instead?

12. What compensated for the Magi's lack of knowing the true God and His Word? What was their ultimate incentive in going on to Bethlehem?

13. What was the traditional and historical significance of each of the three gifts the Magi presented to Christ?

14. Why didn't the Magi return to Herod? What alternative plan did they follow and how did they carry it out?

FOCUSING ON PRAYER

- Do you know anyone whose attitude toward the Lord is like either Herod's or the Jewish leaders? Pray that God would soften and awaken the person's heart and grant him saving faith.

- How is your sense of worship and generosity toward Christ right now? If it is lagging, ask God to reenergize it that you might model the enthusiasm of the wise men.

APPLYING THE TRUTH

Memorize Matthew 2:10–11.

CHAPTER 9
RIGHTEOUS PARENTS

SUMMARIZING THE CHAPTER

Because they were righteous and knew Jesus was the Son of God and Savior, Joseph and Mary obeyed God's Law and testified to Christ's birth by bringing their Son to the temple for circumcision, naming, and presentation to the Father.

Getting Started (Choose One)

1. Today's highly industrialized technological societies are quite pluralistic and offer many different political, religious, and economic beliefs. How does this situation compare to Israel at the time of Jesus' birth? In your opinion, how does a pluralistic culture most challenge the spread of the gospel?

2. Has your family or your spouse's family had a habit of observing any special family customs regarding new babies, anniversaries, graduations, or other milestones? If so, which ones have been most meaningful and enjoyable to you? If your family has not observed such customs, why do you think that is?

ANSWERING THE QUESTIONS

1. Name the three major Jewish factions that were representative of Israel's unbiblical outlook at the time Christ was born. Briefly describe each one's beliefs.

2. What basic beliefs and practices characterized righteous Jews like Mary and Joseph?

3. When and to whom did God first introduce the rite of circumcision? What did circumcision symbolize?

4. What did Jesus come to earth to do concerning the Law (Matt. 5:17)? What besides His circumcision illustrates that intention?

5. What difference did Jesus' perfect obedience make concerning His work at Calvary?

6. Why was the choice of a name for their son such an easy one for Joseph and Mary?

7. What were the practical consequences of the Jewish mother's time of ceremonial uncleanness and personal purification? What kind of spiritual reminder was intended for those times?

8. What did the special presentation of Jesus in the temple area indicate? What did it not mean? Was that presentation any more necessary than circumcision or baptism? Explain.

9. What options did Mary have regarding what to bring for her purification sacrifice? What did her choice indicate about her economic situation?

10. What greater reality did the sacrifice for purification preview?

FOCUSING ON PRAYER

- Pray that the Lord would keep you focused on walking with Him and freed from competing worldly influences that seek to distract and divert.
- Ask God to help you be as obedient and faithful to the details of His commands as were Joseph and Mary.

APPLYING THE TRUTH

Do a study on the subject of God's saving nature. Look up the passages cited in this chapter, and by means of a topical Bible or concordance, trace out other passages. What are the key words, concepts, and recurring themes in these verses? What picture do they portray of God's salvation? Ponder what you've discovered and ask God for opportunities to apply those principles and share them with others.

CHAPTER 10
SIMEON'S EYES OF FAITH

SUMMARIZING THE CHAPTER

Simeon's testimony to Christ demonstrated the supreme joy of a righteous Jew to whom God fulfilled His promise and providentially directed him to meet the Messiah. God used him in a brief but significant way to affirm the truth that the infant Jesus was indeed the Christ.

Getting Started (Choose One)

1. Do you often stay up late or get up early to meet somebody or see something? When you do, what motivates you most to do that? Why? Which one was your most memorable or rewarding?

2. What would you vote for as the most revolutionary new concept or invention to appear in your lifetime? Or in the last one hundred years? Why?

ANSWERING THE QUESTIONS

1. How did the meaning of Simeon's name fit so well with his lifelong pursuit?

2. What truths about Simeon's character are synonymous with the description of him as "just and devout"?

3. What was one of the major sources of Simeon's Messianic hope?

4. How was Simeon's hope and desire a precursor to the apostle Paul's? What passage demonstrates this?

5. In what ways did the Holy Spirit work in Simeon's heart and life? Were those phenomena completely new? Why or why not?

6. What did the continual excitement and anticipation of looking forward to Christ do for Simeon's motivation?

7. What other occasion coincided with Simeon's finally meeting Jesus?

8. What was the practical and theological connotation of the expression "depart in peace"?

9. What prophetic utterance by Simeon went beyond the Messianic testimony of Zacharias, Mary, and Joseph? Why was it so shattering and revolutionary, even for believing Jews?

10. What statements from Isaiah should have prepared people for Simeon's statement about the Gentiles?

11. What final words by Simeon tempered the euphoria Jesus' parents felt at his initial pronouncements? Why were those final words directed more at Mary than Joseph?

12. What response to Christ did Simeon predict most Jews would have? What was so painful about that to Mary and other believing Jews?

13. What affliction of soul and spirit did Simeon foresee for Mary?

14. Who, in a sense, is placed on trial by Simeon's prophecy? What does that mean? What is the only response that people must make to this?

FOCUSING ON PRAYER

• Pray that the Lord would make your anticipation for Christ's Second Coming as deep, heartfelt, and persistent as was Simeon's for His first coming.

- Thank God for His sovereignty and faithfulness that, in the midst of the fulfillment of Simeon's prophecy about opposition to Christ, some are yet turning to the Savior in faith and repentance.

APPLYING THE TRUTH

Try memorizing the two stanzas of the Charles Wesley hymn quoted at the opening of chapter 10. Meditate carefully on the key words and phrases. Look up related Scripture references that support and enhance the sentiment of the hymn. What truths impress you the most and in what practical ways might you apply them?

CHAPTER 11
THE SUPERIORITY OF JESUS CHRIST

SUMMARIZING THE CHAPTER

A survey of Hebrews 1 provides a fitting conclusion to a volume on the birth of Jesus Christ. The writer emphasizes the significance and superiority of His person and work by reminding us of Christ's divine nature, His role as Creator and Redeemer, and His glorified position at the right hand of the Father's throne in heaven.

Getting Started (Choose One)

1. Should believers take strong stands on extrabiblical convictions and issues (politics, economics, lifestyle preferences the Bible doesn't address)? Why or why not? Have you ever stood firm on a controversial issue (excluding Christianity) that was a distinctly minority position? What was your position and how did others respond?

2. In addition to Hebrews 1, what New Testament passage on the nature of Christ do you find particularly helpful and encouraging? Why? How has it benefited you in the past?

ANSWERING THE QUESTIONS

1. What vantage point is most important for us in considering the birth of Christ? Explain.

2. What was the writer's main purpose in penning the letter to the Hebrews?

3. Why had many in the Jewish community not placed their trust in Christ?

4. What tangible concepts do the expression "at various times" refer to?

5. The Old Testament is basically what kind of revelation? What is its primary theme throughout?

6. What was familiar to Jews about the phrase "in these last days"?

7. According to Hebrews 1, what is the first aspect of Christ's preeminence? What familiar laws support that? How does this aspect affect believers?

8. What is the second aspect of Christ's preeminence (Heb. 1:2)? What does the term "worlds" refer to in this verse?

9. What does "the brightness of His glory" (Heb. 1:3) indicate about Jesus? What practical ministry can that result in through believers?

10. Name the fourth element of Christ's preeminence and cite the ancient creed of the church—along with the relevant phrase from the creed—that affirms this truth. What does Paul teach about this doctrine?

11. List the fifth aspect of Jesus' preeminence and name the principle He uses in implementing it. How is that principle divinely worked out?

12. What is the sixth manifestation of Christ's preeminence and why is it so crucial?

13. In what way was Christ's sacrificial death most obviously superior to the Old Testament animal sacrifices? What had to be true about His sacrifice for it to be effective?

14. What is the final preeminence of Christ (Heb. 1:3)? When did it take effect? What does it signify now?
15. What were the essentials of the Jews' attitudes and beliefs about angels?
16. Why did the writer of Hebrews use the Old Testament to argue for the superiority of Jesus over the angels?
17. From Hebrews 1:4–14, write down the five ways in which Christ is superior to the angels. In two to four sentences for each point, explain its meaning and significance.

Focusing on Prayer

- Spend some time thanking God that He oversaw the progressive revelation of the Old Testament that prepared the way for the complete presentation of Christ in the New Testament—and that He did so in a way that preserved for us a full and accurate picture of our Lord and Savior.
- You may know a believer who is new or immature in the faith and struggling with understanding the nature of Jesus Christ. Pray that through Hebrews 1:1–3 they would come to love and embrace His preeminence.

Applying the Truth

Memorize at least one of the following passages: Psalm 2:8; John 8:12; Romans 8:16–17; Philippians 2:9–11; Colossians 2:9–10; Revelation 19:6–7.

CPSIA information can be obtained at www.ICGtesting.com
Printed in the USA
LVOW091228140812

294280LV00002B/6/A